beginner's guide to

THE WESTERN HORSE

A Handbook

By NATLEE KENOYER

1977 EDITION

Published by
Melvin Powers
WILSHIRE BOOK COMPANY
12015 Sherman Road
No. Hollywood, California 91605
Telephone: (213) 875-1711

To MONTY

Who opens the doors
and sweeps off the thresholds.

COPYRIGHT © 1962 BY NATLEE KENOYER

Third printing, April, 1969

The Western Horse was originally published
in 1962 over the imprint of Duell, Sloan and Pearce,
an affiliate of Meredith Press

Printed by
HAL LEIGHTON PRINTING CO.
P.O. Box 1231
Beverly Hills, California 90213
Telephone: (213) 983–1105

Library of Congress Catalog Card Number: 62-15459

Manufactured in the United States of America for Meredith Press

"Reprinted by arrangement with Hawthorn Books, Inc."
ISBN 0-87980-271-5

Foreword

SINCE the end of World War II the "horse business" has enjoyed boom years. There have been many reasons for this, I believe. Most Americans were in somewhat better financial circumstances; we had a little more free or leisure time on our hands; there was a swing toward urban and rural living, away from the crowded big cities; and the country as a whole enjoyed a sort of "western holiday" through television, movies, musicals, and advertising.

Riding clubs sprouted and flourished, organized trail rides bloomed, and horse shows blossomed as never before. Stall facilities at country fairs, state fairs, and even major livestock shows had to be enlarged, even though many of these facilities were built during the so-called "horse era."

Dude and guest ranches were in clover, and riding stables were scouring the country looking for gentle horses to handle the ever-growing riding classes. Manufacturers of western wear and gear saw the wave coming and dug in to meet the demands. Even the automobile, which supposedly sounded the death knell for Old Dobbin, is now pulling a sleek trailer, hauling the horse to distant places for shows, sales, rides, race tracks, and rodeos.

FOREWORD

It wasn't all sunny, however. With the roses there are always some thorns. There was a shortage of horseshoers and large-animal veterinarians and, while there has been much scurrying and activity in these fields, the shortage still exists.

The biggest problem, though, was education. Almost a whole generation had given more thought to horsepower than to horses and when their children got horses and ponies there were many questions and few answers. In too many cases there were no answers or partial answers or, in the worst cases, *wrong* answers. Moreover, this shortage of knowledge and information still exists, even though there has been much scurrying and activity to get the questions answered.

This book will help to fill that gap. It will be a salvation to parents in answering the multitude of questions brought forth by the young riders in their family; and the parents, too, will profit. Anyone with a horse will be happy to have such a book in his library. To a horse owner the answer to one single problem—on care, feeding, breaking, training, riding gear, equipment, or facilities—is well worth the price of this or any book.

This book represents far more than the time it takes to sit down and write it. The information and answers contained in it are the results of many years spent with horses and riders, and the training and instruction of both.

Dick Spencer III, editor
The Western Horseman Magazine
Colorado Springs, Colorado

Contents

Foreword   vii

Introduction   xi

How to Buy a Horse   3

Contracts and Agreements   12

Stabling Your Horse   18

Getting Acquainted with Your Horse   27

The Psychology of the Horse   36

Your Horse's Health   44

How to Ride   51

Training Your Horse   66

Bad Habits   79

Etiquette   86

Trail Riding   93

Horse Shows and Gymkhanas   99

Glossary of Terms   107

Introduction

The original western horse had its beginning as a Spanish horse of war, then as a horse trained to work cattle on the ranchos of Mexico, Texas, and the Southwest. American cattlemen further developed the western horse.

The original western saddle horse had but one function, and that was working livestock. Some horses were highly trained in the art of cutting out cattle, others as calf-roping animals, and the ordinary horses were found in the strings of night herders. Today the western horse exhibits his abilities in many fields. His life is a far cry from that of his ancestors on the ranchos. Before selecting a western horse the horseman should determine the purpose and choose a type to fit the particular need. However, this does not mean merely owning a horse and going through the act of riding. Yes, there is much today that goes into the making of a unit, and it isn't all on the horse's back. There is nothing more beautiful than the coordination of a rider and horse. Too many people buy a horse with no idea of how to take care of it. The desire is there but not the understanding. A lot of thought must go into the care, the grooming, and the training as well.

INTRODUCTION

If attention is not paid to all these things the owner is disappointed, the animal is frustrated, and neither the owner nor the horse is helped or happy. So many books on the technical side of riding have been written that the everyday problems and the detailed care of the horse have been neglected. These questions and the answers are what the new horseman is looking for.

It is certain that the person who owns, loves, and cares for one particular animal for any length of time, sufficient to learn the animal's character, will derive ten times more pleasure if there is complete understanding.

In this day of planes, fast cars, and streamlined ships the horse still holds a great fascination for us. Horses still perform important work even in this mechanical age, but the pleasure horse has tripled in number in the last five years, and the real worth of this animal is now being appreciated. Thousands go to the races, polo matches, rodeos, and horse shows. Those who own a horse can tell of the delightful companionship. It is a challenge to the horse owner, solving the problems, curing bad habits, and spending hours in training for the show ring. But the horse is only as good as its rider.

Horses have personalities. The traits and characteristics that make the animal an individual must be recognized and developed. The best approach must be studied. When an amateur climbs into a saddle and picks up the reins it is rather a sad thing to see, and the sympathy is most certainly with the horse. It is also sad to see an animal confined to a small corral without room to trot and with a little hay thrown any time the owner thinks of it; to see the ribs begin to show and the coat lose its gloss; to see a manure-laden corral with flies annoying the animal. This book is purposely written in the hope of doing away with these things.

Remember, the horse is a somewhat helpless animal inasmuch as he depends on his owner to care for him, make all his decisions, and do his reasoning. The horse is timid and nervous by nature. He is not normally vicious but will fight what he does not understand. He can think of only one thing at a time. He can reason a little but makes up for the lack of reasoning by cleverness if given the chance.

I have written with some detail on the selection of the proper horse, the best stabling for the money at hand, the care and training of the individually owned animal, and the treatment of bad habits. I have broken down the cost of feeding and the necessary equipment.

For the lover of horses who wants an animal of his own this handbook on the western horse will bring a better understanding of what is needed from both horse and rider. The primary rules for learning to ride and to train a colt are set forth. With the help of a parent these chapters should guide a child toward a reasonable and pleasant mount.

This book is offered as an aid to buying, handling, and maintaining a horse and to understanding how a horse thinks and why he performs as he does. Finally, through these pages I hope to increase the love for the western horse to the extent that the reader will want to have and to care for his own. And may it encourage the horse lover to try the pleasure and satisfaction of being his own stableman and trainer.

How to Buy a Horse

Buying a horse is actually the simple procedure of exchanging dollars and cents for an animal of your choice. But buying an animal suited to your abilities is a difficult task. Before looking for a horse decide what use and purpose the horse will serve, for pleasure, for breeding, or for showing. Each of these is in a different category and requires a different kind of animal. However, you may be fortunate enough to find a combination of all three attributes. It is true the "outside of a horse is good for the inside of a man." This, however, will not be true if you buy the first horse you see. Also, don't fall so much in love with a horse that you can't sell it to buy a better one. This sounds like a heartless piece of advice, and it is in a way. It is not the money involved in buying a horse that might prove unsound, but in the attachment you form so quickly. To be forced to destroy an unsound animal is like losing part of your family. It doesn't take long for an animal to entwine himself around your heart. Also, every horse becomes old far sooner than the rider. This is why it is so important to buy the right one. Shop around and look at many before you decide. There are two ways to buy a horse—from a private owner and from an auction.

There are many different types of horse auctions. And, like buying from an individual, some are more reputable than others. Perhaps the main drawback in going to the auction is that you don't have the opportunity to inspect the stock thoroughly, or you seldom try it before you buy. If you know the reputation of the auction or the selling individual you stand a better chance of getting a fair deal.

Most reputable sales now publish catalogs giving pictures, pedigrees, and information about the consigned horses. A breeder may have a complete dispersal sale, which means, as the name implies, that he will sell all of his stock. He may be going into another business, retiring, or working on another breed. Sometimes a ranch will have a dispersal sale to dispose of young stock and to place an oversupply of certain bloodlines in different parts of the country. Sometimes older stock, of fine bloodlines, will be sold to make room for younger stock, of equally fine pedigrees. There are invitational sales where top quality stock is offered to a few selected breeders. There are specific breed auctions where only registered stock is sold. These are quality sales where every consigned animal is inspected by a veterinarian and sifting committee. This protects the buyer from unsound animals. Sometimes a two-day auction may be held to sell grades one day and purebreds the next. Sometimes breed associations will sponsor an auction such as the Thoroughbred and Quarter Horse to sell yearlings and two-year-olds. Auctions sponsored by a registry association will set up certain standards. If it is a production sale it is used to present the best of a breeder's or association's breeding program or to cull out the bad ones. However, at this type of sale, attention is called to blemishes and unsound horses are usually eliminated.

Then there are the weekly or monthly auctions held locally by a sale barn where everything and anything is sold. Here, whether you pick up a bargain or get stung, depending upon the reputation of the sale yard or your own knowledge of horse flesh, is where the usual pleasure horse is sought.

If you go to an auction of this type be sure to take a horseman with you. Remember, you buy the animal "as is" and there are no refunds. Most stockmen selling horses will do so in the fall of the year so as not to feed them through the winter. The prices are lowest in December and January, starting to rise in February. Horses are taken to this type of auction either for a quick sale or if there is unsoundness in the animal. The average price of good horses—by that I mean breeding, training, and beauty of form—does not change, but the market for what we call "trading horses" varies with the seasons. Mainly, these consist of mediocre stock of no particular breeding, aged animals, has-beens, and stock that someone must sell quickly for some reason or other. Yet, some good horses are sold at the horse auctions run by sales companies.

An experienced horseman may be able to detect unsoundness better than you can. Don't be afraid to buy a thin animal, however. A horse can be put in good shape in thirty days with good feed. It will be thin for three reasons. First: because of lack of proper feed. Second: because of worms. Third: bad teeth. For any other reason there would be a definite sign of illness and the animal would not be allowed in the sale yard.

In dealing with the private owner there should be a guarantee as to the health of the horse. If you are in doubt it is advisable to have a veterinarian examine the animal. No reputable dealer will ever refuse to permit such an examination. Blemishes do not always mean a horse is unsound. A horse is judged by appearance, and while blemishes do not interfere with the performance of the animal they do reflect the owner's care of the horse. Cuts and abrasions do leave a blemish sometimes; however, such injuries can be taken care of so as not to leave scars. Unsoundness is anything that causes a malfunction of the part of anatomy of the horse such as ringbone, heavy scarring, faulty conformation, or a pulled muscle. An experienced horseman will be able to find faults that you would never see. He will look first for soundness in sight, wind, and limb. He will understand personality traits and degrees of being spoiled.

Consider these tests before you buy a horse:

1. Look at him from a distance and examine his build as a whole. This is called conformation, and each breed of horse has certain characteristics that identify him by form. The animal should carry his head well and be neatly put together.

2. Check for soundness. Run your hands up and down his legs. Look for an unexplained lump or sign of soreness.

3. Test his vision. A horse should blink when you wave your hand in back of his eye.

4. See whether or not he leads in or out of the stable easily.

5. Watch saddling and bridling. See if he is uneasy when cinched. Some horses are afraid of a girth, caused by too tight a cinch. Notice whether or not he is bridle shy, touchy

6

about the ears; whether he opens his mouth to receive the bit.

6. Have the owner ride the animal so you can see how he handles. Watch whether he stops easily, reins well, backs, and has an easy gait. Have the owner work the horse to a gallop. Try to determine if he is speed crazy. The owner should guarantee the safety of the animal as to training. Also, note whether or not there is excessive breathing, noise with the breathing, and flanks that heave spasmodically.

7. Most important! Ride the horse yourself. Is he smooth in the walk, trot, and canter? Does he shy? Is he spooky? Can you start and stop him? Is he too spirited for you to handle? Does he switch his tail constantly? Can you ride him away from the stable? A tail-switcher means that the animal has been pushed too fast in training and indicates nervousness. Usually a horse that has been trained by a woman will not like a man rider, or will be uneasy with a man on his back. Sometimes this works in the reverse. Many times it is because of the handling of the reins. A man is normally heavier handed than a woman. However, this depends on the horse and the rider in the main, but it is something to consider in buying a horse that has been privately owned by one person for some time.

8. Don't buy a stallion. He may look good in the movies but is not practicable in real life. He is likely to be unpredictable and should be managed only by an expert horseman. He belongs, mainly, on the breeding farm. You'll find just as much spirit and animation in a good mare or gelding and far less trouble.

No horse is perfect, but whatever faults are present you must decide whether or not they may be eliminated with some training. Many times all a horse needs is work. Horses also respond to owners. They have their likes and dislikes. Personalities clash just as between people. Whole personalities have changed with ownership.

Be sure the animal is suited to your own capabilities. And, once again, don't buy the first horse you see. Somewhere is a horse suited to you. Two things are important: the age of the rider and of the horse, and the experience or lack of it in both rider and animal.

One must equal the other, rider and animal, because no matter how well trained the horse, if the rider does not understand this training, then the horse will not work well. And a good horse can soon be ruined by a poor rider.

There is no need to be an expert to find pleasure with a horse, but both animal and rider must know the basic principles of horsemanship to be compatible. Too many prospective horse buyers are entranced by the animal's appearance and forget to find if the horse is suitable. If the horse cannot be managed by the rider he is no good for the new owner no matter how beautiful he is.

If only a pleasure horse is desired, an animal from nine to sixteen years old will prove a safer mount for a child than a younger animal. The pleasure horse is the most reasonable to buy and maintain. You should find one for about $100 to $350. Try to find an animal that has been privately owned, is gentle and reasonably trained. Everyone who desires to own a horse should take at least a year of instruction in riding. In buying a mature horse there will be less danger than in finding one that becomes easily excited; he will have more patience, and will tolerate reasonable use by children.

HOW TO BUY A HORSE

Even a gentle horse is apt to become mean if parents allow children to aggravate it hour after hour. Parents must be ready to teach a child compassion and respect for the animal's rights. Teasing should not be permitted, and certain hours for riding should be planned. A parent who is not willing to do this may be buying trouble.

As with every other sport you can either get by with little expense or spend a small fortune. Everything depends upon what you want from your horse and the type of riding you are going to do. Remember, owning a horse is a pleasure and comes under the head of entertainment. When you think of the cost of keeping it, compare it with other forms of sport and entertainment costwise.

There are many good, useful horses who will never win a prize for beauty but will be loyal and safe and pleasurable. With common-sense care there should be no more cost than routine feeding. A parent should remember this: a child's horse, dependable, safe, affectionate, and healthy, is worth thousands of dollars in the peace of mind he gives, even if it is a fifty-dollar animal in actual money. Many horses are usable until twenty years of age, a few even older. For the very young child there is nothing better than an old horse to start on.

For the person who wishes to show in the ring a more specialized animal must be sought. First, decide what category of showing you wish to enter. Usually a well-trained horse can be used in most of the performance classes. The same animal can be used for Western Pleasure, Equitation, and Trail-horse Class. Depending on the animal and its disposition, this same horse can be used in the Stock-horse

Class. This, however, is a difficult class and takes a good horse and good hands.

Surely no one is going to try to show a horse without knowledge of horsemanship. To do so would be a waste of time and money because of the competition. The correct riding clothes and the right kind of saddle are important. An animal of good breeding and good conformation is important also. And most important of all is the willingness of the rider to work. To go into the show ring seriously takes many hours of practice and an effort at perfection. The horse must be kept in top physical condition and well groomed.

A good show animal is quiet and steady in the ring and just animated for the requirements of the class. A fiery animal has no place in western showing. There are two courses to follow in buying a show animal. A horse can be bought by reputation. This is one who has already collected trophies and ribbons or one that promises to be a winner. These horses are usually schooled and trained by a professional. The second way is to train your own horse.

If there is enough knowledge of horsemanship there is no reason why an owner cannot train his own horse. The experienced horseman usually prefers to buy a green colt and train it from the beginning. This, however, takes a long period of time and is a good idea only if the exhibitor is willing to wait.

In the ring good sportsmanship is a must. The crowd is quick to boo the rider who takes his loss out on the horse. Therefore much depends on whether you want the rigors of the show ring or you want only the pleasure of equine companionship. Horses have their good days and bad days so at times will not work so well as they're able. Decide what you can pay, and try to find the best animal to fit the price you can afford. Conformation costs, and so does training. Try, also, to find the most for the least. This is "horse trading," but, as with everything else, you usually get what you pay for.

Contracts and Agreements

THE buying and selling of horses should be handled in as much of a businesslike manner as any other transaction. "Horse trading" has been applied to every kind of transaction because of the many ways in which you can be misled in a sale. More than one sharp merchant who never came near a horse has been called a horse trader. Many a lifelong friendship has failed because of a verbal agreement. It may seem harsh to be particular with a friend, but all agreements should be thoroughly discussed and understood before any deal is undertaken. If possible, make a contract and put the agreement in writing with both parties signing. There will then be no doubt and no chance of saying, "I thought you meant . . ."

Even "friends," or "friends of a friend," have "just the right animal for sale." There are many reasons for getting rid of a horse. *A man must sell a horse and just wants a good home for him and will accept a very reasonable figure. Naturally, the animal is worth more.*" Beware of such bargains. Because when the horse does not turn out right the "friends of the friend" will suddenly become quite for-

getful about the animal and won't remember saying anything. Don't ever commit yourself until you have a chance
to examine the horse thoroughly. There are many ways of
making a horse seem to step out sound. In some instances
sellers have been known to shoot Novocain into a painful
leg so that the horse can walk without a limp.

When you buy an animal, have the seller write a descrip-
tion of it and the markings. If buying a papered animal
(registered), the markings are on a chart on the back of the
pedigree. See that the contract states that the animal is
sound and as advertised. A man bought a purebred show
horse for his daughter for $3,500. They worked the animal
for a week and noticed he constantly stumbled in the figure
eight. A veterinarian was called and an X ray showed an
old fracture down in the foot among the small bones. In
this case the money was returned and the horse went back
to the previous owner because the animal had been sold as
sound. The seller knew about the injury, but the animal
had not been used for months and did not limp in the walk.
It was a case where the seller thought the affliction might
not show up for some time, maybe too late to look like an
old injury.

Another animal was accepted on a sale, but the final contract was not signed or did any money change hands. The
following day the animal came down with a case of extreme
colic and died a few hours later. In this case there was no
transaction consummated so the seller was the loser.

A horse may be bought "on time." However, anything
happening to the animal after delivery does not change the
contract and the horse must be paid for, as with any contract.
The seller, on payment of a deposit, delivers the animal and

there his responsibility ends. For example: a mare in foal was sold. The pregnancy was verified by the veterinarian before delivery of the mare to the new owner. The contract, signed by the purchaser, agreed to pay fifty dollars a month until paid in full. Two days after delivery the mare broke out of her corral and was struck by a car. There was no apparent injury, but when the time came for foaling there was no colt. The owner did not want to pay the balance. In this instance the seller was protected by a signed contract and by the veterinarian's previous examination. The seller was not responsible for the animal's care or condition after delivery.

Should the horse become mean after the sale he is still the responsibility of the purchaser. Perhaps a lack of knowledge or mishandling is the cause.

Agreements can cover more than just buying a horse. Many times when you have an extra stall your friends may want to stable their horse with you. Usually they agree to buy their own hay, but you will find you are taking all the care of the animal. Also, the first thing that may happen is that they run out of hay and you will be feeding the horse for nothing. It is much better to set a boarding price because nothing but trouble ever comes of any other kind of verbal agreement. Figure that your time is worth something. Why should you clean a stall and corral daily for nothing?

Should you board your horse at a stable, the owner is not responsible for accidents or for the illness in your horse unless direct neglect can be proven. If your horse breaks down a fence, tears up his manger, kicks a hole in his stall, or jumps a fence, the resulting accidents cannot be blamed on the stable owner. Such acts expose nails and cause splintering which in turn might result in abrasions, contusions, and broken bones. A well-cared-for animal is not prone to illness and is normally healthy, but he may get such things as colic or a cold from the carelessness of the horse owner and then become ill later.

If the animal becomes unmanageable when out riding, throws you, and then causes damage, you are responsible. If you allow anyone to ride your horse and he falls, causing an injury, you can be sued. If the rider can prove the animal dangerous, he can collect. Don't allow strangers to ride your horse unless you are well insured. It is not a good idea to allow a nonrider to sit on your horse. Although the rider may be at fault, should an accident occur it can cause a great deal of hard feelings and possible law-suits.

Sometimes an agreement is made that a horse may be used for the keep. Make this agreement definite and in detail; how much and what kind of use. A riding school agreed to board a horse free for use in teaching students. One day, without a word, the owner came and took the animal away, leaving six students stranded without a horse to ride. Even this arrangement seldom works out satisfactorily, because just about the time the boarder decides to ride, the owner comes and upsets the plans. The owner has the feeling, "After all, it is my horse and I'm letting you use it for the keep.... I surely ought to be able to ride him when I wish."

Many times a buyer will wish to take the animal home to try. This is never a good idea. The rider is strange, the place is strange, and the animal cannot be expected to work his best. The prospective buyer will be able to find too many things wrong with the animal and will then attempt to "deal," figuring that having the animal in his possession you will not want to haul him back again. However, if this is done, be sure to have a written agreement. The animal can be injured or become ill from wrong care and it is next to impossible to collect for a dead horse if there has been no agreement. Anyone buying a horse will be able to tell in a few rides of a short length of time whether or not the animal is suitable or whether he can handle him. Don't allow the buyer to ride more than two or three times in order to make up his mind. Some people may take this opportunity to ride a horse without any intention of buying.

Perhaps we should say a word also about equipment. New equipment, whether it be gear for the horse or trailer, costs a great deal of money. Unless you know the borrower well, don't lend. It seems that people seldom bring equipment back in good shape, especially that used on and around horses. Don't lend a good trailer. Offer to drive yourself to deliver an animal. If it is a good friend, and you are used to accommodating each other, this is well and good. If strangers ask about trailering a horse, charge them according to the going rate in your area. Usually trailering costs so much a mile, with maybe a minimum set figure for short hauls. It is difficult to generalize, but prices range from five to ten cents to twenty-five cents a mile for more than fifty miles. Some local haulers for distances under fifty miles charge a dollar a mile. Freight rates are by the hundredweight and you furnish the crate or the seller furnishes the crate with return.

At almost any big auction sale arrangements can be made to transport an animal to your home or someone may have extra space in his trailer and will be glad to offset his own expenses by hauling for you. Professional haulers are almost always available, but it is advisable to insure your animal if you consider him valuable. Horses loaded in an open truck can be hauled extremely cheaply but you may have three months of veterinary bills to pay to get your animal back into good shape again. For any distance van hauling is the best because the vans are built to accommodate the animal. Whatever method of hauling you choose there should be a complete understanding as to hauling rates before the animal starts on his journey to avoid any possible misunderstanding.

Stabling Your Horse

Before you bring your horse home you should be prepared to stable him. It is better to buy your saddle and bridle after you have the horse in order to get tack that will fit and something that suits the type of animal you have purchased.

Stabling depends on the part of the country in which you live. Naturally where there is extreme cold and snow the horse should have a fairly warm place, free of drafts, to feed. However, don't pamper your animal. The horse is a hardy animal and nature provides a coat heavy enough to survive any temperature. The animal will fare all right as long as he has plenty of feed and water.

You can go all out and build a picture barn with Dutch doors and the like, or just a makeshift lean-to, depending on how much money you have to spend. A horse can get along just as well with a lean-to against a garage or any other building—something to protect the manger from the weather and the horse from wind. It will not be necessary to hang a door on the corral side of the stable because the animal will then have the privilege of going and coming

18

as he chooses. Double doors on the outside on the entrance side are good, so the horse can look over the bottom door section and yet be protected from drafts if the weather is cold. You will find that a horse will stand in the driving rain with his tail toward the downpour, but wind will almost always drive him inside the stall. A drop door just above the manger will make feeding easier without having to go inside the stall.

The stall should be well drained. Many horse owners like shavings or straw bedding. However, it is not necessary, and only raises the cost of keeping the horse and certainly takes more care. A wood floor is acceptable but can be noisy. It is easy, however, to keep clean by sweeping and the use of dehydrated lime. This floor can be well drained if the spaces between the studding are filled with small gravel. The presence of the gravel filled to the level of the boards so they rest on rock makes a steadier floor because there will be no give between the studding. By using gravel you can get by with 1 x 12's of redwood or any local wood instead of 2 x 12's.

The best floor is clay. A four-inch layer of red rock or gray slag, sprinkled and then rolled, makes a firm footing, not slippery, easy to rake, and drains well. It can easily be repaired by adding more clay and rolling with a lawn roller.

If you have a half acre or more your horse should have a small corral adjoining the stall, at least 20 x 20 feet. If you have only room for a corral and can make it a large one, then your stable need only be 10 x 10 feet with a corner manger. It is a good idea to draw a plan for stable

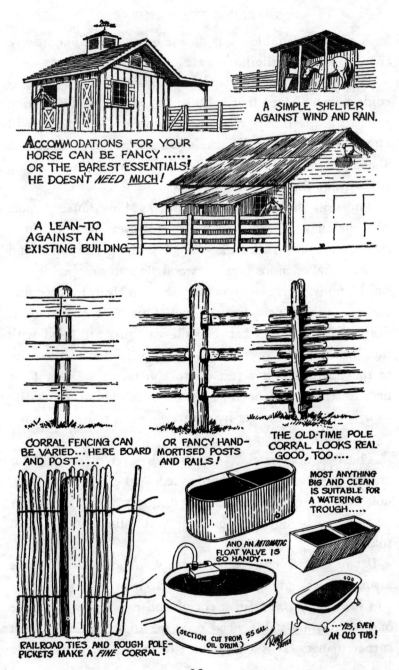

A SIMPLE SHELTER AGAINST WIND AND RAIN.

ACCOMMODATIONS FOR YOUR HORSE CAN BE FANCY ...... OR THE BAREST ESSENTIALS! HE DOESN'T *NEED* MUCH!

A LEAN-TO AGAINST AN EXISTING BUILDING.

CORRAL FENCING CAN BE VARIED... HERE BOARD AND POST .....

OR FANCY HAND-MORTISED POSTS AND RAILS!

THE OLD-TIME POLE CORRAL LOOKS REAL GOOD, TOO....

MOST ANYTHING BIG AND CLEAN IS SUITABLE FOR A WATERING TROUGH.....

AND AN *AUTOMATIC* FLOAT VALVE IS SO HANDY....

(SECTION CUT FROM 55 GAL. OIL DRUM)

...YES, EVEN AN OLD TUB!

RAILROAD TIES AND ROUGH POLE-PICKETS MAKE A *FINE* CORRAL!

20

and corral that will give you an idea for a more compact area to care for your horse and equipment.

Look for used lumber—1 x 6 or 2 x 6 rails are good. At the same time, look for metal nosing. Used nosing can usually be had for the asking. Nailed to the inside edge of the boards and painted the same color as the fence, it will insure an unchewed fence indefinitely. Nosing can also be nailed to the edges of fence posts. Horses appear to have a taste for some woods and will chew a post in two in a few days. If you live in a part of the country that has trees that grow tall and straight and about four inches in diameter, these will make an excellent rail fence. Usually rails that have been dried thoroughly will last indefinitely and the horses will only be able to pull off the bark. An owner of a grove may allow you to thin the trees for the rails. They should be ten to twenty feet long. Some woods will work well above ground but will quickly rot if used as posts. Railroad ties that have been discarded make substantial posts and usually have been treated against rot. Never agree to barbed wire. Many a good horse has been ruined by deep cuts, not to mention constant scarring.

An electric fence is reasonable and simple to install but it will not always hold all horses. It is easily grounded and easily broken. If you have enough land it is better to put your horse in the corral at night and turn him into the pasture during the daytime. It keeps him out of mischief at night and gives him something to look forward to. The animal's water should be in the corral.

A double laundry tub (chipped or damaged seconds) can be bought from any plumber for about a dollar. This can be filled with the hose, or water piped and a faucet used, or one half of the tub boarded over to cover a float such as the type used for chickens. This will insure the horse having constant fresh water. An animal will drink out of almost anything, but it appreciates clean water.

A horse is naturally a clean animal. Many horses will choose a spot in the corral or pasture to place their droppings. Many will never urinate in a stall; however, there are dirty horses just as there are untidy people. A garden rake, a barn broom, and a scoop shovel will make cleaning easy, and a small wheelbarrow will aid in removing the droppings. If you have only one horse, you can dispose of the droppings around the flowers. Or you may designate a place in a corner of the yard where the manure can be put to use later. A little fly spray on the fresh droppings will dispel any flies, and more on the pile will keep them away. If manure is spread out so it is dried by the sun, the flies won't bother it anyway, because they are attracted by the dampness. Also, if the manure is well dried before it is piled there will be almost no odor and there will be no need to spray. As to the odor itself, most people do not object to it, it is not a menace to health, and if you follow the above there will be no fly problem. Horses should not be subjected to flies. The animal is easy to keep clean and should have the privilege of enjoying clean surroundings. The walls of the stable can be sprayed safely every two weeks; use dehydrated lime on all wet spots in the corral or stable. This will sweeten the ground and eliminate the odor of urine. As nearly adjacent to the stable plan your equipment storage.

If you cannot have a tack room then plan a corner of your hay storage for a place for the saddle and bridle. A one-

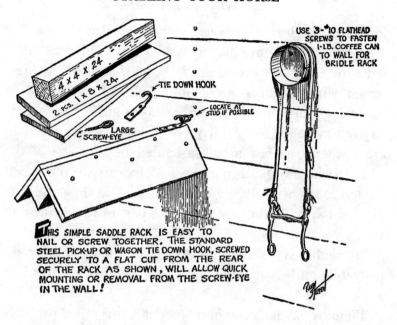

USE 3-#10 FLATHEAD SCREWS TO FASTEN 1-LB. COFFEE CAN TO WALL FOR BRIDLE RACK

4 x 4 x 24

2 PCS. 1 x 8 x 24

TIE DOWN HOOK

LOCATE AT STUD IF POSSIBLE

LARGE SCREW-EYE

THIS SIMPLE SADDLE RACK IS EASY TO NAIL OR SCREW TOGETHER. THE STANDARD STEEL PICK-UP OR WAGON TIE DOWN HOOK, SCREWED SECURELY TO A FLAT CUT FROM THE REAR OF THE RACK AS SHOWN, WILL ALLOW QUICK MOUNTING OR REMOVAL FROM THE SCREW-EYE IN THE WALL!

pound coffee can nailed to the wall will make a good bridle rack. A wooden rack can be built for the saddle. A clean grain sack kept over the saddle will keep off the dust.

The type of riding you will do will decide the kind of saddle to buy. The McClellan saddle (American military saddle) is good for children. It is said to have one of the best-balanced seats of any saddle. A western saddle should have stirrups that are easily adjusted and are free moving. A lightweight saddle is easy to handle. Be sure the leather is in good condition, neither dry nor cracked. Look at the sheepskin lining to see that it is not too worn, and there should be no loose nails. A small wooden box nailed to the wall will hold your grooming tools. The feed area should be large enough to hold from one to three tons of hay.

The price of hay always goes up in the wintertime, so

it is best to buy your year's supply in June. The hay area should be approximately 8 x 10 feet. This will allow bales to be stacked three deep. Most bales are two- or three-strand wire. It takes twenty-four bales of two-strand to make a ton and fifteen of the three-strand. For years now hay has averaged from thirty-five to forty dollars a ton in areas where the hay must be hauled in. In parts of the country where you can go to the field, hay may be purchased for ten to twenty dollars a ton depending on the type. The kind of hay will also depend on the part of the country in which you live.

Prairie hay is excellent horse feed. It is high in minerals, palatable, and nourishing. It is also less dusty than other hays.

Timothy hay is a good horse fodder if it is raised properly and cut and cured the correct way. It can be too heavy and woody in the stock, and might result in a lot of waste. Too much dust from the pollen can give a horse heaves and broken wind.

Oat hay is an excellent food, but if purchased once a year the mice and rats will eat most of the grain and actually you will be feeding straw, and then extra grain must be supplemented.

Cane hay is raised in Texas and Louisiana with fine results. It has lots of leaves and a big head full of sweet oily seeds.

Johnson grass can also be fed. It is coarse hay, usable if cured properly, but once started it can take over the farm.

Blue grass is recognized as one of the finest grasses for pasture feeding and is especially recommended for breeding farms because of its mineral content.

Alfalfa is an all-around feed. Rarely do you have to feed grain, with the exception of mares in foal. It is high in protein. It is said to be heating, but in areas where it is raised the work horses eat nothing else and riding stock does extremely well. Feeding the horse will depend on the animal himself.

Usually the Department of Agriculture will be glad to suggest a combination of dry-land pasture for your horse if you have room to grow supplementary feed. Normally, a short-backed, big-barreled animal with well-filled-out rumps will make good use of his feed.

A horse should be fed the minimum that will keep him from losing weight. If you are working your horse daily, then he should have a feeding of prepared horse feed every day or so.

A little-used horse can get by on red oat hay alone, but a well-rounded diet for an active animal should include alfalfa and a prepared feed. Many fine high-protein foods in pellet form are being used today. A horse who has access to pasture or lawn cuttings will be that much better off.

It is difficult to say how much a horse will eat, but the average saddle horse will eat one pound of hay for every hundred pounds of body weight. A three-strand bale of hay will last a horse nine days. This means your horse will eat three and one half bales a month or three and one half or four tons a year for approximately nine dollars a month if you use the figure of thirty-five dollars per ton. A working horse should have a prepared horse feed. Most feeds of this kind have vitamins, minerals, and enough worm medicine to keep down parasites. There are many horse feeds on the market today. Try them all, and find one that benefits your horse the most. Feeding on schedule and keeping your animal clean will cut down the cost of upkeep. Routine is important, because the horse is a creature of habit and it should influence the horse owner.

Getting Acquainted
with Your Horse

BEFORE anyone can become a successful horseman there must be an understanding between owner and animal. The horse is in many ways like a child. He forms habits readily and whether they are good or bad is up to you. The good habits must be developed and the start of bad ones stopped at the first sign. You must build confidence. Establish in your horse's mind your method of approval and whenever he does your bidding always use the same manner of compliment whether it be reward or voice.

In the beginning all the potential horseman sees is this beautiful animal with the big brown eyes, lovable and endearing. But the horse is a complex animal with intense emotions often as deep as a human's. As you watch him, put yourself in his place and try to think as he thinks. Step down to his level so you may understand his fears and frustrations.

Take your time getting acquainted and don't expect the impossible of him. It will take a few days to become used to new quarters. Don't make demands of him that are beyond his physical and mental capabilities. If you find the animal has some bad habits, work methodically, step by step, as the habits present themselves. A horse is never too old to train provided he has not been broken in spirit or hurt physically.

The horse's upper lip is his finger. He uses it to examine everything. Before presenting something new to your horse, let him feel it with his lip. Don't rush him. Let him take his time. You will be surprised how quickly he will accept what is requested. A horse and rider work best as a unit.

Because the main quality of this unit is understanding a rider will get the most from his horse if the animal has full confidence. He fears disfavor, so we work on his craving for approval. The best way to become acquainted with a horse and to discover his little idiosyncrasies is by grooming. Take much time at this, and stop to talk and pet him. He will not understand the words, but it will accustom him to the tones of your voice. Have a few pieces of carrot in your pocket so he will look to you for tidbits. However, don't feed him sugar. The animal becomes so fond of it that he will get overanxious and be apt to nip at you in an effort to get more. Make your horse feel you mean him no harm when you approach him. You will notice how alert he is at this time because he does not know what to expect from you. Horses often sleep on their feet. Be cautious until you get to know him well.

When you approach him in the stall, be sure he knows you are behind him before entering. Be sure his weight is on the side on which you intend to enter. If he is inclined to kick or if you startle him, you can be safely out of the way before he can change position and kick with the leg on your side. You will find that your horse will relax around you as soon as he is used to your presence and knows how you will act around him.

Take every precaution with a new animal until you thoroughly recognize his likes and dislikes. When walking around his rear, stay close to him. If he should kick, he will only be able to shove you, but if you are two feet away you could receive the full impact of the kick. An animal likes the feel of a hand. Run your hand along his back when close to him. Examine your horse thoroughly to see what condition his coat, head, and feet are in. A rough coat may indicate worms or improper feeding. Examine his feet for small rocks and need of trimming.

A horse's feet should be cleaned well about the frog every day. Carrying your extra weight, a rock lodged in the frog of the foot might cause severe lameness, and there is always danger of a nail. The type of country you live in and where you will be riding will determine whether he needs to be shod or not. Rocky country and pavement demand shoes.

Pasture and soft mountain trails will allow an animal to go barefoot. The feet should be trimmed every three months. If your horse is shod, the shoes should be watched for wear. Ill-shod horses or those forced to wear worn shoes are just as miserable as a person whose feet are not properly cared for. Shoes should be reset or replaced every six weeks at the longest.

Find out what kind of bit your horse has been used to, and if he works all right with it, then buy the same thing. For pleasure riding all that is needed for a well-trained animal is a snaffle or low port curb bit, or you may want

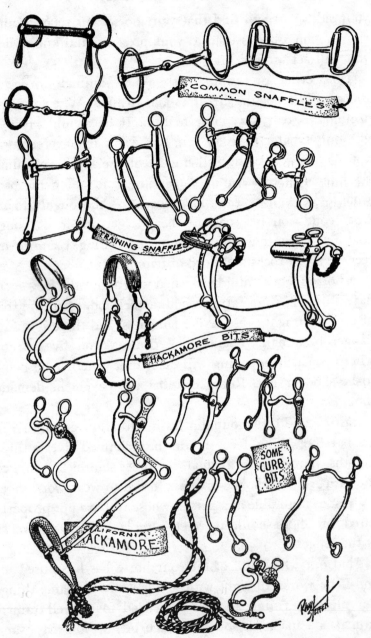

COMMON SNAFFLES

TRAINING SNAFFLES

HACKAMORE BITS

SOME CURB BITS

CALIFORNIA HACKAMORE

to ride him with just a bosal and rope reins. The hacka-more was first used by the Spaniards to teach reining. Raw-hide was woven into a loop, placed over the animal's muzzle, and tied with a hair rope to form reins and a tie rope. A single loop of leather over the top of the head held the bosal in place. The hair rope was tied in such a way that the knot fitted directly under the jaw. It rubbed a tender spot, which made the animal easy to stop to get away from the hurt. Different-size bosals were woven to suit the pur-pose. From this idea came the metal hackamore bits. There are many types of hackamore bits, some severe and some worth little. The Kelly hackamore works as a squeeze bit and will stop the toughest animal. The good point of the metal hackamore is that it will not tear the horse's mouth because it works only on the nose and jaw. Many ropers prefer the hackamore bit. However, don't be in too much of a hurry to change bits. Get acquainted with the animal's way of going and later decide if anything needs to be done. You must get used to him and he must become accustomed to your hands.

Keep your horse haltered when you first bring him home. It is always easier to handle an animal if you have some method of restraint, providing you have him under constant observation. However, when you are ready to turn your horse into pasture, remove his halter and allow him to run free. There is nothing better than a well-fitted halter with which to handle a horse, but too many owners are careless with the way they place a halter on their horse. They either leave it too loose or buckle it too tightly around the throat. A light halter will break easily if the animal pulls back when the leather is caught on a nail or fencing, but a strong, heavy, stitched halter is not easily broken. It is possible for an animal to get his foot caught while cropping grass. It is natural for him to struggle to free himself, and the result could be a broken leg or even neck. Rope halters are cheap, and many horsemen use them, but they are extremely dangerous to leave unattended. Rain will shrink them, causing swelling and distortion of the horse's head, not to mention agony and pain. In tying your horse you should know two knots and when to use them.

First: a slip knot. Never tie a slip knot around the animal's neck. If you intend to use a slip knot fasten it only to the halter. Also, when tying to a fence or rail be sure to tie the horse up fairly short so he will not be able to get his leg over the rope and cause a burn. A bowline knot can be safely used directly around the horse's neck.

Sometimes a new horse is hard to catch in a pasture. If

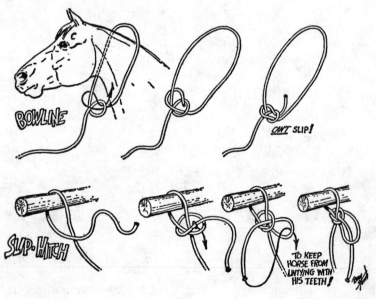

BOWLINE

CAN'T SLIP!

SLIP-HITCH

TO KEEP HORSE FROM UNTYING WITH HIS TEETH!

you carry bits of carrot or apple when you go to catch him you will find he will come to you as soon as he sees you. Don't approach in a hurry. A horse who thinks you are not interested in catching him will soon approach you with the hope of a "handout." If you have taught him to "come," then stop and wait for him. Some like to run a little, to tease, before they decide to come to you. Let him have his fun; it is quicker than chasing him. Don't leave your horse tied for hours at a time. Always tie him while grooming or cleaning his feet.

Every animal should be taught to lift his feet to have them cleaned. All horses have to be taught to balance on three legs while the fourth is being handled. Reach for the pastern or fetlock and shove against the horse to make him put his weight on the opposite leg. Lift and bring the foot into position to see the bottom of the hoof. Hold the hoof in the left hand and grasping the pick so that the pointed end is down, clean out the crevasses about the frog. Watch for small pieces of gravel and nails. In handling the rear feet, after you lift the foot, walk away from the horse, slightly pulling his foot back. This will force the balance on the opposite foot, the ankle joint against your thigh, and the hoof will be easier to manage. Clean the horse's feet before every ride.

Don't bring your horse out of the stall, mount, and trot or gallop off. Give him a proper grooming first. In the wintertime it may seem a waste of time to attempt to groom a heavy coat, but it will make the animal feel better. It will hasten shedding in the spring. A teaspoonful of raw linseed oil in the grain three times a week will hasten shedding and put a layer of fat underneath the skin.

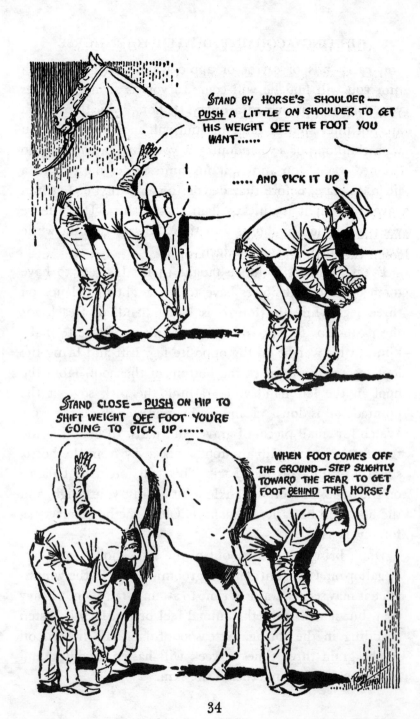

34

GETTING ACQUAINTED WITH YOUR HORSE

After saddling, walk the horse around to get the cinch adjusted and to be sure the saddle is firm. Don't cinch the saddle too tightly. With proper balance a rider can even use a saddle without a cinch, so there is no necessity of making the animal uncomfortable. When mounted, don't start off with a gallop. A horse needs to be warmed up as any athlete should. Be sure to walk the last part of a ride. There is a rule for horses that you walk the first mile out and the last mile in. After a ride, if your horse is hot, loosen the girth and walk him around until cool. Remove the saddle, scrub him well with the rubber currycomb, and brush him down. After a final brushing a flannel cloth is good for wiping the animal's coat and putting a gloss to it.

Your horse is a creature of habit, so keep him happy with a routine feeding schedule. He will not do well if fed at four o'clock one day and seven the next. Remember your horse is dependent on you and your care. Use common sense and you'll both be happy.

The Psychology of the Horse

How many times have you heard people say that horses are stupid, unable to reason, and extremely selfish? But who stops to take the trouble to find out what really makes a horse "tick"? Admitted, there are stupid horses just as there are stupid people, but this large animal is full of fears, emotions, and affection. The answer behind all this is, simply, that horses are most dependent on people. There are many stories of stallions protecting their herds with tricks that only a good mind could manage. Range horses know the dangers they are up against and react much differently than pasture-raised animals.

The domestic horse is protected with shelter, good food, and care by an honest owner. He seldom has to think about more than play or having his own way. His reasoning comes from boredom, the desire to get out of work, and a search for forbidden food. Horses copy each other. If one animal sees another break a fence, raid the hay barn, or find the grain barrel or even open a gate, he immediately wants the same and follows the same procedure to get it.

Perhaps the people who least understand the horse's way

of thinking are the horse dealer, the commercial breeder, and the average stable owner. These people are not sufficiently interested in the animal's personality to care how the individual horse thinks. A horse has a one-track mind, but what he can do with such straight-line thinking would amaze you. Divert his attention and you change his mind. Learn the different expressions of his eyes, his mannerisms, his likes and dislikes.

Watch your horse for an indication of what he is going to do. Actually, an animal telegraphs every move he will make. It is up to the owner to learn to "read" his horse. When an animal is going to shy or buck, the muscles of of his back tense and can be felt through the saddle. The ears tell volumes. Ears stiffly forward means the animal is acutely alert. This means interest, curiosity, or fear. The conditions presented will tell the rider what it means. One ear forward and one back means he is listening for the rider and keeping an ear pointed for something ahead.

Ears laid slightly back means he doesn't like something or doesn't want to do what is asked. Ears laid back flat against the head means the animal is vicious or angry. He will try to fight, either the owner or another horse. Horses have a pattern of thought, and once you know them you learn how they react to different situations. But remember, these big animals are afraid of everything they cannot understand or see. If a horse realized his strength, we would never handle him. But he is dependent on man. This is the secret of handling a horse and making a useful animal out of him.

A horse needs something to depend on. You seldom see him alone by choice. At the racetrack the thoroughbred has a chicken on his stall door, or a goat to share his hay, or a dog to lie at his feet, or a cat to rub against his legs. Sometimes a small pony shares his stall; he may look for a favorite groom who talks to him; often there is a quiet understanding between the trainer and the horse, but . . . there is always something . . . someone.

When a horse becomes accustomed to your presence and your voice he will begin to take on personality. A quiet, authoritative voice that can also soothe and give confidence will win an animal quicker than anything else. The horse may be able to understand only twelve command words, but the tone of your voice will speak many things to him. Although the horse is normally timid, he will develop confidence in you to the point where he will trust you implicitly. I remember having a mare who almost trampled me when she was frightened. If she had been a small dog, she would have leaped into my arms. This big animal thought all she had to do, when she became frightened, was to get close to me for protection. She shied at everything along the roadside. I finally taught her to quiet down when I said, "That won't hurt you." She still danced along warily, of course, but under control. She was still afraid, but the tone with which I spoke the phrase told her that she was safe.

The horse demands attention and craves affection. However, it must be remembered that a horse is made to do things by fear, hunger, thirst, and biological urge. So we use these things to our advantage without forgetting the other requisites that round out the complete picture of the horse, such as attention and affection. He does things only to satisfy his hunger, demands for comfort, and curiosity and attention. He cannot concentrate for long periods of time.

He learns by habit, and, once taught, seldom forgets. His memory is remarkable. It doesn't take him long to learn what reward means. And reward may be food, a show of affection, or a soothing word. Reward will make him more attentive the next time. There are so few ways in which a horse may offer affection, but he will thrive on yours. However, I have had a horse protect me from a dog. My horse circled me, with his ears back, and struck at the dog every time it tried to get close enough to bite me. I was a little afraid of being trampled, but I was more afraid of being bitten by the dog.

Horses are not born mean, but one that is not handled with firmness and understanding can become so. Meanness is too often caused by spoiling rather than by timidity. Naturally, a horse will have likes and dislikes that do not always follow your desires. He is an individual. Let him remain so as long as he is easy to manage and does no harm. Remember, a horse is a sensitive animal with a highly developed nervous system. Stop to think what the average horse endures from rough hands and a bobbing rider who does not know the fundamentals of horsemanship. Can you blame him for fighting back? If he rears and bucks, what other way does he have of voicing a complaint?

Physical punishment should be used only when it is the last alternative. It must immediately follow the action and not a second later. Many times a sharp word will work, but a smart crack with a whip is necessary for biting and kicking. Don't think, however, that a horse's reactions are always from mistreatment. Normally, the animal is lively, mischievous, and full of tricks. He bucks on a crisp morning because he feels good and perhaps hasn't had enough exercise. He nips and kicks and strikes because that is the way he plays. The horse does not realize his own strength, so a playful blow from a striking hoof could kill or maim you. Don't put yourself in a position to receive one. In other words, don't play with your horse. A horse will play just like a dog. I've seen horses grab a hat and run away with it, dashing about whenever you come near. However, any play must be of a safe sort. He must be made to understand that there are certain ways he cannot play with his owner. He will have more respect if he is taught that there are certain things you will not tolerate. Watch for his natural inclinations and develop them. I heard of a horse who walked along with his head down looking for a foot-long stick. Finding it, he would pick it up and then reach around and scratch his back with the stick. We had a mare who liked her tail scratched. She would back to you all the way across the corral and stand waiting to have her tail scratched. Another horse, in the same corral, watched a few times and then started backing in the same way. Seeing a horse backing toward them frightened some of our friends, but this little mare didn't kick. However, horses are great bluffers.

If an animal discovers he can frighten you he will take advantage of the fact and make your life miserable. If you stand your ground and strike him smartly across the nose, when he comes at you with teeth bared, he will stop and walk away foolishly. This refers to a horse you know well and the average horse; the vicious horse is another matter. You must be able to distinguish between the two. Your own mount may not try anything with you but lay his ears back and whirl to kick with strangers. No one can fathom why a horse will like one person and not another. A woman-trained horse may not like a man and vice versa. Unless an animal has been mistreated and teased he will always like and tolerate children. I've seen a baby toddle forward and grasp a mare between the back legs, and the animal didn't move. If an adult, without some kind of warning, had come up behind this same horse he might have been kicked.

A horse is extremely emotional. A happy animal has no problems. A nervous, worried animal will withdraw into himself and appear to take no interest in anything but food. And he will lose weight no matter how much he eats. He will either walk the fence or stand, hour after hour, in a corner with his head down. A definite creature of habit, he wants to be fed at the same time every day. He wants the same stall. He wants the same type saddle used. A horse that has been ridden with a western saddle will balk at the first sight of an English saddle. Everything he meets must be examined by "feel." As soon as the animal is convinced that the offering will not harm him, he will quiet down and accept it.

In the first handling of the foal confidence is the primary accomplishment. Foals are afraid of anything taller than themselves. In getting acquainted with the foal, you sit on the ground. Curiosity gets the better of him. He smells, feels with the tip of his muzzle, tries an experimental bite. It is a plain case of selling the colt on the idea that he will not be hurt. As the colt grows, he will take on definite personality traits. He will want all your attention. A horse is a jealous animal and will fight another horse to keep him away from you. It is not safe to get between two horses who are vying for your attention. A colt will welcome your company any time and will do many things to be with you. A loose rail will invite him to crawl through the fence. Many horsemen will insist that a horse should not be made a pet. This makes a horse a nuisance, they say. A well-disciplined, well-loved horse is never an annoyance. It is a pleasure to see the understanding your horse has. If he is intelligent, he will get into mischief and will figure out clever antics as well.

Ask any horse owner about the animal he's fond of and he will tell you many stories. And these stories belie the fact that a horse doesn't reason. A retired cutting horse stood watching a man on foot trying to corner and catch a horse in a pasture. Finally, after many attempts by the man to reach the horse, the cutting horse trotted forward and cornered the animal himself and kept him in position until the man could walk up to him. The cutting horse is the intelligencia of horsedom. He is directed by his rider to a certain steer and then cuts that steer from the bunch without further reining, preventing the animal from returning to the herd by anticipating every move. He works entirely on his own until the rider directs otherwise.

There are always the gate openers. The first thing a horse usually learns about his new home is the position of the gate. Most stock gates have a slide bar for easy handling. One mare discovered she could pull the handle with the tip of her muzzle. Somehow the top of the handle was broken off even with the top rail of the gate, making it necessary to grasp the handle below to pull the bar back. In two days the mare had solved this problem for herself. Finally, a hole was bored just back of the handle and a nail shoved through the hole, preventing the bar from being pulled back when in place. The mare discovered by jiggling the gate that she could work the nail out of place, and the gate opening continued. It was necessary to put a chain around the gate with a snap before it remained closed. But a dozen times a day she would go to the gate to try the handle to see if anyone had failed to snap the chain. But these acts of mischief can be avoided and give the horse owner a chance to brag about the cleverness of his horse.

Understanding the horse in the early days of civilization was almost unheard of. Training a horse was a simple matter. The animal was caught, mounted, and ridden until exhausted, and then kept worn down until he finally accepted his lot. There are stories of the courageous animals that offered more than ordinary resistance and refused to give up, even in exhaustion. Some finely bred animals often fought to the death rather than submit. Finally, when the horse became the principal means of transportation, it was found necessary to develop good horses and devise ways of breaking and training so they would be safe and efficient. Some early trainers had a special gift of training, and it is these who, maybe unknowingly, discovered the psychology of the horse. And so for you to understand your animal you must search for instincts and natural inclinations and frame your training and understanding on these natural instincts. The most satisfied owner will be the one who appreciates what the horse is up against and makes allowances. And the big thing is patience.

Your Horse's Health

Every horse owner should know a few facts about first aid and the general health of a horse; the care that can be managed by the owner and when to call the veterinarian. There are many instances when a minor injury can be taken care of by the owner, but for the more serious ailments and accidents there are several aids that can be given before the veterinarian arrives. Too many times the wrong treatment is given, resulting in ugly scars, or a horse is moved when he should be kept still, or allowed to lie down when he should be kept moving.

Probably the commonest of everyday problems is concerned with cleanliness. A dirty, constantly wet stall will invite a fungus called thrush. It is characterized by a foul odor and decomposition of the tissue about the frog of the foot. A few drops of butter of antimony in the crevices will usually relieve a light case, and a good cleaning of the stable area will prevent further trouble.

Rope burns are too commonly caused by improper tying of your horse. If severe, you may have to lay your horse up until the burn is healed. Cleanse the wound and apply gentian violet and a healing powder. Do not grease, and, above all, keep the flies away.

Diarrhea is a condition with many causes. Sometimes it is caused by a change of feed. If caused by worms, they must be expelled, and your veterinarian will prescribe. Sometimes an overheated animal that has been allowed to drink water will develop diarrhea. It is usually not a permanent condition, but the actual cause should be determined.

Idleness and fat are the worst enemies of your horse. Allow him at least an hour and a half to eat his food. Don't exercise him too heavily after a meal, or it may cause colic.

Colic: It is important to recognize the symptoms. Colic can also be caused by sudden changes of feed, irregular feeding, or damaged feed. Sometimes new oats or new hay causes trouble, or colic appears if a horse is fed too soon after being tired and hot. In spasmodic colic the pain comes and goes. The horse may throw himself to the ground and roll and kick. The animal must be kept moving and on his feet. Walk the horse until the veterinarian comes.

Fractures: Many animals are destroyed because of a broken bone that has not been discovered until too late. A horse has many small bones that, when broken, only cause the animal to go lame. When no reason for lameness can be discovered, then the horse should not be moved until the veterinarian has made a thorough examination. Given proper care, minor fractures can be treated, either by splinting or casts, thus giving the horse back its usefulness. Fractures of a more severe nature can be set if discovered before the horse threshes around. If the animal cannot be confined, there is danger of splintering and crushing the broken ends to the point of being beyond setting.

Swelling: This can be a symptom of foreign bodies, such as splinters, glass, or infection itself. This includes viruses, glands, infection with pain on contact, heat, sore throat, and, in an advanced stage, drainage. An infection should never be neglected. Let your veterinarian make the diagnosis and prescribe the treatment.

Azoturia: This ailment, sometimes known as black water because the urine becomes dark, red-brown in color, is caused by a malfunction of the muscles. This malfunction is due to the lack of proper nutrition activated by exhilarated exercise when the animal is not used to it. The symptoms are heavy sweating, stiffness, and rigidity. At the first sign, keep the animal on his feet. The symptoms are: the horse will start off with unusual vigor. Within a half-hour he will begin to sweat profusely, knuckle over in the hind fetlock, and perhaps even fall in his tracks. If the animal is urged on after the first symptoms appear, the condition will be greatly aggravated and death follows quickly. At the first signs keep the animal on his feet. If necessary to move the animal, walk him slowly to a stall and see that he is not moved. There should not be a draft. Blanket the horse and keep him warm. If the horse gets down, there is little chance for recovery. One attack makes the horse subject to another attack so that as soon as the veterinarian gives permission the animal should be exercised every day. No oats should be given, and feeding must be carefully administered.

Foaling: There is a thrill to looking forward to the arrival of a foal. However, it is a frightening experience to realize that the mare has started foaling and is unable to complete the delivery. Lack of precaution might mean the loss of both mare and foal. When the foal is in sight and the mare appears unable to complete the delivery, keep her on her feet and moving. See that she has a large area to walk in. Constant walking will delay the heavy pains until the veterinarian can arrive.

Gashes: Nonbleeding. If a cut is made in the muscle it is not apt to bleed. The first thought is to apply medication of whatever happens to be on hand. So many gashes have been burned with too strong a medication and the tissue has sloughed away, leaving an ugly scar. It is important to keep the wound clean. Use soap and water, and cover to keep the flies away. The veterinarian will treat the wound properly before suturing.

But the important factor to remember in any of these emergencies is quick thinking and a cool head plus a knowledge of first aid. Not only will this help your horse but your veterinarian will appreciate your knowledge.

In an older horse you may notice a dropping off of weight. This may be because of teeth that are too long and are cutting into the gums. Horse's teeth continue to grow throughout their lives. The teeth do not always wear down equally and thus lose the grinding surfaces. Sometimes sharp corners will develop that cut the cheeks. The inability of the horse to masticate properly soon shows in an undernourished appearance. When the veterinarian is called, he will file these teeth and trim them down to normal size. This is called "floating the teeth." Once your horse is comfortable again, he will pick up in weight.

Every stable should have a medicine chest.

1. Bandages. They can be made of flannel or old sheet-

ing six inches wide and six feet long. Keep rolled and fastened with a large safety pin, ready to use.

2. Absorbent cotton. For swabs, for washing eyes, and cleansing wounds. Never use against an open wound, as it will stick to the tissues.

3. Epsom salts. For infections and sprains.

4. Vaseline. To use around a wound to keep it clean and prevent loss of hair.

5. Gentian violet. Disinfectant for cuts.

6. Rubber syringe. Large-size ear syringe for irrigating wounds.

7. Healing powder. To dust over cuts.

8. Butter of antimony. Used for thrush. If this medication gives off a smoke, it means thrush is present.

9. Argyrol 5 per cent. Use in eyes. Keep reasonably fresh.

10. A can of hoof dressing. To prevent cracking hoofs.

Watch for accident possibilities and prevent them. Don't be afraid to improvise. For example: Your horse has cut across his pastern with a broken glass jug. An artery is cut. Use a roll of bandage against the wound, or wrap a small block of wood or a stone with gauze and press it against the wound. Wrap tightly with bandage. Continue to wrap until the bleeding stops. This is called a pressure bandage. This bandage should be watched to be sure it is not pulled too tightly. Immediate swelling will indicate this. Watch for infection. It is indicated by heat, swelling, and pain on touch. If the leg remains normal, you may presume it is free of infection and the bandage should remain undisturbed for about eight days. Now, a word about pressure points which would indicate a pressure bandage. Pressure points should be

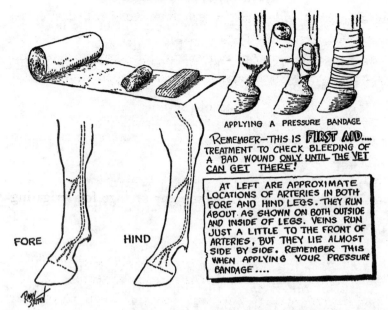

APPLYING A PRESSURE BANDAGE

REMEMBER—THIS IS FIRST AID....
TREATMENT TO CHECK BLEEDING OF
A BAD WOUND ONLY UNTIL THE VET
CAN GET THERE!

AT LEFT ARE APPROXIMATE
LOCATIONS OF ARTERIES IN BOTH
FORE AND HIND LEGS. THEY RUN
ABOUT AS SHOWN ON BOTH OUTSIDE
AND INSIDE OF LEGS. VEINS RUN
JUST A LITTLE TO THE FRONT OF
ARTERIES, BUT THEY LIE ALMOST
SIDE BY SIDE. REMEMBER THIS
WHEN APPLYING YOUR PRESSURE
BANDAGE....

FORE   HIND

found between the heart and the wound. Usually in arterial bleeding pressure is placed on these points. This would be difficult on a horse in most instances. The pressure would have to be placed and treated as a tourniquet and relieved every twenty minutes. So, let us say, that on all legs, from the knees and hocks down, the pressure bandage as described above may be used.

You will hear many terms for different types of unsoundness, and it will take experience to recognize them. Perhaps the following will help you recognize a few of the more common ones.

Bone Spavin. Any bony enlargement on the bones of the hock.

Bog Spavin. Any inflammation or swelling of the soft tissue of the hock.

Capped Elbow. Enlargement at point of elbow.

Curb. An enlargement below the point of the hock.

Heaves. Forced and labored breathing.

Hernia. Also termed rupture. Tissue protruding through an abnormal opening.

Hygroma. Soft swelling of the knee.

Knocked-down Hip. A fracture of the point of the hip.

Poll Evil. A swelling or draining sore in the region of the poll.

Quittor. Infection of the lateral cartilages.

Ring Bone. A bony enlargement around the bones of the pastern.

Shoe Boil. A running sore at the elbow.

Side Bone. Ossification of the lateral cartilages.

Sinus of the Withers (fistulous withers). A swelling or draining sore in the region of the withers.

Splint. A bony enlargement in the groove formed by the splint and cannon bones.

Stringhalt. A peculiar jerking of the hind leg when walking or trotting.

Sweeny. A shrinking away of the shoulder muscle.

Thoroughpin. A soft, puffy enlargement in the web of the hock.

Toe Crack. A split in the front part of the hoof wall.

Warble. Fly larvae in the hide. Usually along the back. After removal it may lay the horse up for thirty days.

Wry Neck. Crooked neck.

Common sense should tell you when an accident or ailment is beyond your ability. Keep your fences and stable area clean and in repair, watch for loose boards, nails, and sagging wire fencing. And remember your veterinarian is only as far away as the telephone.

How to Ride

You often hear people say that they have been riding since they were three years old, or they were practically born in the saddle. Simple logic will belie this. No child of three years has enough coordination or strength. However, children do have a natural balance but no particular rhythm. Every sportsman knows the necessity of coordination, balance, and rhythm.

There must be coordination between the legs, hands, and body in moving a horse forward. For example: to move the horse forward you release the tautness of the reins and shift the body forward. If you shifted your body and pulled back on the reins, you would be asking the horse to stop and go at the same time. The reins, however, act as a control to keep the horse from moving out faster than the rider wishes. Horsemanship has rules of procedure just as any other sport, and in order to get the full enjoyment from a horse the owner should know the basics of horsemanship.

Before you buy a horse there should be a year of lessons, not only to learn the fundamentals of riding but to learn how to conduct oneself around an animal and the stables.

Without instruction you pick up a lot of bad habits. It used to be common practice to throw someone into the water to teach him to swim. In self-taught riding you may be able to ride a horse you are familiar with, but put yourself on an animal inclined to be stubborn or one that hasn't been ridden for some time and you will be grabbing for leather and your apparent accomplishments will suddenly disappear. Not only will you be embarrassed by your own inadequacies but the horse will recognize the lack of skill and take advantage. Yes, indeed, there is more to riding a horse than the mere act of sitting on his back.

Riders can be placed in three categories, as can horses. The rider who goes on trail rides at the usual mountain resorts need only be capable of sitting in the saddle. This rider is called a passenger. The horse has been trained to keep his place in line, behind a certain horse, never gets out of a walk, and follows to the end of the trail and back again. The fact is, you couldn't blast one of these horses out of his place in line with a pound of dynamite.

The second type of rider is the one who frequents riding academies. The rides are for an hour, and the horse knows exactly when this hour is up and will return to the barn whether the rider is ready or not, and usually at a dead run. This type of rider is called a gunsel. If he is lucky enough to remain in the saddle during the run, he believes he is a good rider. These poor horses usually have hard mouths, from amateurs pulling on them, their legs break down from cantering on pavements, and the stable string is constantly being changed because of the condition of the horses. Most academy owners try to buy horses that won't get out of a walk because they last longer. Then, of course, there is the expert and the person who takes lessons. The expert can spot a phony by the lack of correct horse jargon and by the way in which a person approaches an animal. He doesn't have to see them ride. An expert shows his horsemanship, the amateur talks it.

Horsemanship is a science. If we lived a hundred years we would never learn all of it. But there are many phases, and once you have learned the basics you choose the category you wish to follow. And strangely enough every horseman believes his category is the best. The first category is the pleasure horse, with which this book is mainly concerned. In pleasure riding, after the basics of horsemanship are learned, there is nothing to do but enjoy your horse, the companionship, the personality, and the affection that come of owning a personal mount.

Breeding is a business and concerns the improvement of a strain, and exhibition usually follows this phase in order to bring the stock in front of the public. Horse shows offer many categories for showing: Jumping, Saddle Seat, Three and Five Gait, Harness, Western Pleasure, Equitation, and Western Trail, Stock Horse, Cutting, Rodeo, Gymkhanas, and Halter classes. There is a place for everyone from the most expensive horses and tack to the animal of questionable breeding that has talent for games or trailing. Once you have started into horsemanship the way is open in any direction your talents or desires may take you. The opportunity is there, and it depends on what you want to put into it.

Even though it may take years to become an expert horseman you can have fun learning each lesson. Each bit of knowledge and accomplishment will make you eager for more, and each lesson will become more interesting. In riding, coordination, balance, and rhythm become a habit. Watch a horse suddenly shy with an experienced rider. The horseman's body works automatically with the motion of the mount, his hands control the horse's head, and the animal is brought back into position without too much effort.

An uncontrolled horse will do as he pleases. If the inexperienced rider gives the wrong cue, the horse will obey without question, even though it is poor judgment. How many times have you heard people say, "This stupid horse won't go." Believe me, it isn't the horse who is stupid. It is the ignorance of horsemanship showing quite plainly. There is a slogan all horsemen know well, "It is always the rider, never the horse." It is so easy to blame the horse.

A good horseman knows he must do the thinking for his mount because the animal is trained to follow cues and do whatever he is directed. The careless, inconsiderate rider will always be with us, the showoff, the overconfident person without a shred of compassion who thinks only of how fast he can go. For this type of rider the only safe horse is a dead one.

It is well to remember that most of the time a horse is only as safe or as good as the rider on his back. For example: any good horseman knows a horse cannot buck unless he gets his head below his knees. He must collect himself for a buck. If a rider becomes frightened and pulls on the reins, the horse may rear and go over backward. The animal is not rearing because he is mean, he is rearing because the rider is pulling him up and the bit is hurting his mouth. He goes up to get away from the pain. When a horse rears, the rider need only throw his weight forward and the animal will be off balance enough to have to go down on his front feet. Ninety per cent of accidents can be the fault of the rider. A good knowledge of horsemanship will almost entirely eliminate accidents.

There are many schools of thought on how to learn to ride and many methods are taught, but the fact remains that the basic requirements are the same, balance, rhythm, and coordination, and without these three, in some degree, you cannot learn to ride. Everyone develops a style because of the way the body is built. A stout person will not ride the same as a long-legged thin one.

When you start lessons, the first thing that will affect you will be a tinge of fear when you climb on the horse's back. You have to get used to the height from a horse's back. You cannot learn to ride as long as you have any fear, because it makes you tense and there is no place for tenseness on a horse's back. There is little danger of falling off during the beginner period because you will not be allowed out of a walk until you have learned to sit. However, every horseman falls off sooner or later, and the falling is not so bad as the anticipation. You may be thoroughly jarred but rarely hurt. It is usually the experienced rider who falls, and this is because he rides well enough to become careless with his balance.

In mounting, the horse should be taught to stand still. The American Horse Shows rule book says: *Take up the reins in the left hand and place hand on the withers. Stand, facing rear of horse, grasp stirrup leather with the right hand, and insert left foot in stirrup and mount.* This type of mounting will work better for a short person and, of course, if you intend to show, the rule book should be fol-

USE THOSE REINS TO MAKE YOUR HORSE STAND UNTIL YOU'RE SETTLED IN THE SADDLE !!

TWO WAYS TO MOUNT YOUR HORSE

ABOVE: FACE THE SADDLE, GRASP MANE WITH LEFT HAND, HORN WITH RIGHT..... STICK LEFT FOOT IN STIRRUP AND PUSH YOUR BODY UP WITH YOUR RIGHT FOOT!

BELOW: FACE TOWARD HORSE'S RUMP, GRASP MANE WITH LEFT HAND, TWIST STIRRUP TOWARD YOU WITH RIGHT HAND, AND WHILE HOLDING IT STICK LEFT FOOT IN — GRAB HORN WITH RIGHT AND USE RIGHT FOOT TO PUSH YOUR BODY ABOARD !!

lowed. However, there are many ways of mounting, and some local areas may have different rules. Wherever you show, follow the rules of the region. Many people mount from the side, facing the saddle so they may watch the animal's head. If a horse "cow-kicks," it is better to face the back of the animal. If the horse "bites," face the saddle, but this can also be taken care of by tightening the far rein so that the animal cannot get his head around. If the animal is inclined to move before you get into the saddle, tighten the near rein so that the horse will be forced to come back around you. In showing, an animal will be marked down if it moves while mounting and also for bad manners. Many riders like to grasp the reins and saddle horn together and, with leverage, hop to the stirrup and then into the saddle. Some even ignore the stirrup altogether and swing into the saddle from the ground. These are in the same category with those leaping over the rump of the horse and landing in the saddle. Your own prowess and ability at showmanship will govern your manner of mounting. You're always safe, however, to follow state and national rules.

The center of balance is maintained in the position of the legs and feet. When they are in position, you are forced by your own muscle coordination to sit properly. You sit straight but not stiffly in the saddle. Tuck the tailbone well down into the tree of the saddle. The cantle of the saddle is like the back of a chair. It is for support, not to sit on. Pressure against the cantle would put your weight behind the center of the saddle. Such a distribution of weight works a hardship on the horse because the main portion of the body would be over the animal's kidneys. The weight should

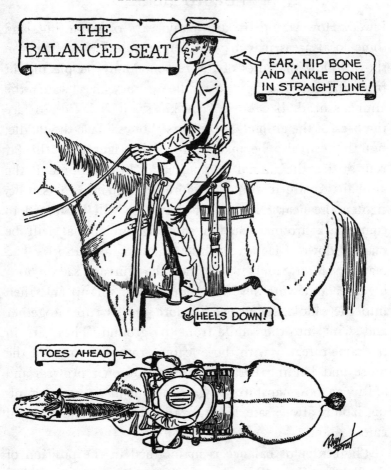

be more toward the withers and put more onto the shoulders of the horse. You should be able to draw a line from your ear, touching your hipbone, to the ankle. Legs should hang straight and slightly forward to the stirrups. The stirrups should be just short enough to allow the heels to remain lower than the toes. The body should always appear comfortable, relaxed, and flexible. The weight of your body should be on the ball of your foot with the toes up and the heels down, taking the brunt of the weight. If you look down, your knee should cover the sight of your toe. The inside sole of your boot should be pressed down on the inside of the stirrup, making the outside of the stirrup slanted toward the horse's body. The toes should be pointed straight ahead. The thighs and the lower leg should maintain necessary pressure and should be in close contact with the saddle.

Remember, you are riding by balance so there should be no forced pressure with the knees. Pressure will come automatically as needed to maintain balance. Perhaps the most pressure is used when jumping a horse when the rest of the body must "follow through," but it is used only during the actual act of taking the rail. Maintaining the feet in the correct position will become a habit as will the balanced seat and the proper handling of the reins.

In repose, arms are in a straight line with the body. The arm involved in holding the reins should be bent at the elbow. In western riding the reins are held in the left hand. The American Horse Shows rule book suggests that the hands should be around the reins. However, here again the manner of holding the reins may vary with the region. In California the reins are held somewhat like an ice-cream cone. Putting the thumb down, you grasp the reins so they enter the palm of the hand by the little finger and come out of your fist over the thumb. They are held in this manner because sometimes just a turn of the wrist inward is enough to stop a horse. The arm hardly moves; there is only wrist action. The most common method outside of California is to separate the reins with the forefinger. This is done to keep the reins from slipping, causing uneven reins

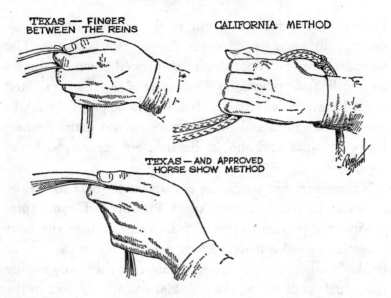

TEXAS — FINGER BETWEEN THE REINS

CALIFORNIA METHOD

TEXAS — AND APPROVED HORSE SHOW METHOD

as leather against leather will slip. Some hold the reins in the position of shaking hands, with the reins passing over the palm, holding with the thumb. If you intend only to pleasure ride, hold the reins the way they benefit you and aid you best in controlling your horse. If you intend to show in western classes, study the manner required by the rule book in your area. The reins are also held in the left hand to leave the right hand free to open gates, swing a lariat, etc.

The reins should be held several inches in front of the saddle horn and about three inches above the withers. The reins should be loose enough to allow the horse the opportunity of following cues but taut enough to maintain control of the animal's head. When you have learned the feel of the reins, your fingers, wrists, and arms will be relaxed and flexible, giving or taking slack as the movements of the horse's head demand. A "feel" of the reins comes only with experience, and every horse's head is different.

Some horses need a firm hand while others can be ridden with a loose rein. You will find yourself balancing with the reins, and the result will be that your mount may continually stop. It takes a few weeks to learn to sit without giving thought to each position of seat and legs, but as you feel your balance improving, sitting will be more comfortable. Don't allow your body or legs to become stiff or let your heels fly up. If you can't remember to keep your heels down, tie a string to your ears and to the toes of your boots. If your feet get out of position, see what happens to your ears. Remember that an improper seat not only destroys your balance but also eliminates the control you have over your horse. But use the balanced seat as the correct form of riding and use the reining to get the best results from your horse. Learn them well.

The reins are the "telegraph lines" to the horse's head. Western horses are neck reined. When turning the horse to the right, move rein hand to the right, causing left rein to touch the left side of the horse's neck. He is trained to move away from the rein pressure. Brace your feet slightly in the stirrups, touch a heel on the turning side (right), and lean slightly, with the body, to the right, and press lightly with the left leg. Measuring from the ears to the withers, strike a middle line on the neck. Lay the reins against this area to turn. Reverse the procedure in order to turn to the left. At first exaggerate your movements so that the horse will "feel" them. As you improve, your cueing will become smoother and only a slight aid will be needed to move the animal in the direction desired.

To stop the horse, shift the weight slightly back and pull back lightly, then release the reins. The stop should be balanced, and if the horse does not stop, pull harder, forcing the animal to an abrupt halt. By pushing slightly with the balls of the feet and squeezing with the knees, the horse will learn to stop without so much pressure on the reins. If the horse does not stop well with reasonable pressure on the reins, he should be retrained. The reason for releasing the reins when the cue is first given to stop is because constant pressure on the reins means to "back."

To back the horse, the chin should be in and a series of short, easy pulls on the reins will back the horse, a step at a time. The rider's weight should be back. Move the horse forward a few steps after backing. This teaches the animal to expect a forward move and will prevent unnecessary backing.

You learn one gait at a time, and it is wise not to attempt to progress until each step is properly learned. You will be using hands, legs, weight, and voice to control the horse. The aids or cues act together in coordination, each aiding or correcting the use of the other.

Perhaps the hardest part of learning to ride is to move the horse. The tendency of the rider is to "kick." A slight touch of the heel may be necessary in the trot and canter, but shifting the body forward should be sufficient to move the horse into a walk. Use caution in "clucking" to the horse as it may affect other mounts in company. The action of the reins and body should move simultaneously. The shoulders should be erect but relaxed. The legs from the knees down along with the feet should be firm and balanced on the ball of the foot in the stirrup tread. If the body is relaxed, the weight will be well about the hips, so when this weight is shifted forward the animal will feel the movement through the saddle. If the animal does not move at once, lay the rein across the neck, forcing him to take one step and then follow, quickly, with the cue again. If the action is firm enough, the horse will move.

Most beginner riders are afraid they will hurt the horse by being rough. A 1,000-pound animal is not likely to be hurt by firm handling. Being too easy will make the horse sluggish and he will not work if he thinks the rider can't force him. Remember, a good horse will step out in a swinging walk, and for trail riding there is nothing like a "good walker." When you have the horse moving in a walk, it is time to learn to trot.

The trot is not a comfortable gait unless the horse is well collected. It is preferred that the western horse either walk or canter when working. However, in the western trot you sit down in the saddle. The balance must definitely be maintained on the balls of the feet, but the rest of the body must be relaxed. Allow the shoulders to take up the jolt of the trot. Pick up the horse's head with the reins until the trot becomes an easy jog. If you become the least tense you will find yourself popping in the saddle. When someone complains of having a sore rear it is because he has gripped constantly with his knees and was stiff in the saddle. Perhaps the most common fault in trotting is to allow the hands to bob up and down, thus loosening and tightening the reins. This will make the trot rough. The cue for the trot is firmer than for the walk. The position of the body in the saddle is a little farther forward than in the walk. The position of the body is still to maintain balance, so when you feel the center of balance once more you will know you are forward enough.

The canter and the gallop are the same movement but differ in speed. No one gallops a horse unless he is racing or if necessary to make speed. A well-trained western horse is known for its "rocking-chair" canter. It is a comfortable gait if the horse is collected and in the correct lead and the rider is well balanced. The rider must "sit" well down in the saddle but not too far back. The body from the hips up is relaxed to the point where the waist feels slightly as if it is swiveling back and forth. Actually, if the balance is correct, the body will move only with the motion of the saddle and be a part of it. The elbows are well in. Don't flap the arms like a sea gull. It not only looks bad but spoils the center of balance. Don't tighten the thigh muscles. Keep a firm leg and ball of the foot in the stirrup and allow the upper leg and thighs to relax against the movement of the saddle. The body will be slightly forward, and as the speed increases will tend to go farther forward to maintain even balance. At a full gallop the weight of the body should be off the saddle, putting it on the knee and ball of the foot. The horseman will ride with a shorter rein and the hand will be extended farther over the horse's neck. The hands must be light on the reins, adjusting themselves to the movement of the horse's head, controlling but never jerking or pulling.

Should you allow your legs to go back and your toes to point downward you will have lost control of your horse. You will be pulling on the reins to get your balance, which will put a hard mouth on your horse. One should never gallop unless he is proficient in the canter. In learning the canter the rider should be aware of leads.

By leads the horse is said to be cantering on the left front and back leg in advance of the right. In cantering around a circle the animal should be on the inside lead. The correct lead is important in maintaining good balance and maneuverability for the horse and a comfortable ride for the horseman. If the back lead is not in coordination with the front lead, it is possible for the horse to have no support, which might result in a fall. All horses are right- or left-handed, so the lead will come to the accustomed side. Without weight on its back an animal will normally change leads, but not always with a rider. All horses have to be trained to use one lead as well as the other.

To take the lead to the left, turn the horse's head slightly to the right and shift the weight to the left. It is a matter of throwing the horse's balance to the desired lead. If it is difficult to put the animal into the correct lead, follow the above directions on a curve and the horse will go into the correct lead with more ease. When the animal is in the correct lead, straighten his head so he is going straight ahead. To take the right lead, just reverse the above. Like everything else, this takes practice. Riding is not impossible to learn, but those who have good coordination will find learning easier. Always work to improve, and the results will be well worth the effort.

Training Your Horse

To TRAIN A HORSE properly, the cost can be in the amount of time consumed. If you wish to buy a well-trained horse you must expect to pay for this training. The ability to train depends on knowledge and experience, but anyone with the basic knowledge of horsemanship can train a horse. Today people want a gentle-broke animal. However, the new owner must be warned not to buy a horse that has been started by an inexperienced horseman. Usually this is the reason for selling. The animal may have been so misused that it cannot be retrained and the result may be much trouble and possibly danger.

Any professional trainer taking on a new horse will ask what has been done. The time it takes to undo bad training will be added to the usual training price, and also the disposition of the animal will be taken into consideration before acceptance. If the new owner has found a gentle colt, unspoiled, there is no reason to forego the job of training if a careful step-by-step plan is followed and if each lesson will not be hurried.

Too many animals are ruined by being pushed into

training when they have not been prepared for it. First, the trainer must be quiet-spoken and patient. Even a sixty-pound child can start a colt under saddle as a yearling. There is no age at which the colt can't learn. However, there will be more satisfaction with the training if the gentling can be started from the day of foaling. If the foal can become accustomed to being handled daily, the child will have little difficulty when the actual training starts. Many horse owners dislike the idea of buying a weanling because they feel there will be too long a wait before the horse can be ridden. But the feeling of accomplishment can be rewarding as you watch a young colt develop under daily handling, and the time passes quickly if you are interested. It is up to the parent to decide whether the child is capable of training, under supervision, or whether to buy an aged animal for the child to play with.

The young owner must be impressed with the importance of moving quietly and slowly around a young colt. The baby first must get used to the feel of hands. To hold the animal gently, slip the left arm under the colt's neck while the right arm encircles the rump.

At first the colt might try to free himself, but he will soon learn to stand quietly. The next step is to pat the colt over the whole body, scratch around the ears, and rub his back. The colt must tolerate this handling before taking the next step.

Handling the colt's feet is in the next lesson. Keeping the right hand on the halter, the free hand should be run down the hind leg, grasping the lower part of the pastern. Lift the leg slowly, moving it forward and back. The colt may lose his balance and jerk his foot. Try again and again, until the colt learns to balance. Pick up each foot every day and move it about until the colt does not object and learns to balance. It is important to praise the colt after each successful move.

Start talking to the colt so he will begin to understand the tones of the voice. The colt will start to enjoy each lesson because of the petting and the praise, and eventually there will be no sign of fear. About this time the colt will try to play. Colt play consists of striking, biting, and kicking. These antics are cute in a tiny foal, but as the animal grows and becomes stronger they can be dangerous. Now the colt must be taught what *no* means.

Limit each lesson to periods of ten minutes, gradually increasing the time as the colt grows older. He will lose interest if the lesson is too long. No matter what age, never work on a lesson longer than twenty minutes for the best results. This appears to be the animal's limit of concentration. Be sure to finish the lesson with the act the colt knows well. Never quit on a failure.

The average horse learns about twelve words. These must be used as commands. The colt will learn quickly that a sharp "no" means something is wrong. Say the word sharply. If the colt tries to bite, strike him lightly on the nose and say "no." For the first ten days of the foal's life he has no teeth. He chews on anything and everything just as a puppy does. Baby teeth are sharp, so the foal must be taught he must not bite people.

The same words should be used for each command, such as "hold it," when the colt is to stand quietly; "come," to bring the colt to you; "easy," if the colt becomes restless and impatient. A halter can be put on the colt when he is two

THESE ARE BUT A FEW OF THE MANY METHODS OF

HALTER BREAKING

TYING A GOOD STRONG INNER-TUBE BETWEEN TWO POSTS OR TREES PREVENTS A COLT FROM HURTING HIM-SELF — NO MATTER HOW HARD HE FIGHTS.... AND IT WORKS BY ITSELF WHILE YOU'RE BUSY WITH SOMETHING ELSE!

SLIP HITCH

— BOWLINE KNOT

THIS BREAST-HITCH METHOD WORKS ON ANY SIZE COLT — AND IS PERFECTLY SAFE. A COLT LEARNS TO "HUNT THE SLACK" QUICKER WITH THIS METHOD THAN WITH 'MOST ANY OTHER. BE SURE TO USE A LARGE DIAMETER SOFT COTTON ROPE — AND *ALWAYS* TIE OFF WITH A SLIP HITCH!

THIS WORKS WELL WITH THE VERY YOUNG FOAL. AN ASSISTANT LEADING THE FOAL'S DAM AHEAD OF YOU WILL MAKE THE LITTLE FELLOW LESS EXCITED, AND WILL GET HIM ACQUAINTED WITH HANDLING MUCH QUICKER. A SLIGHT TREMOR OF THE FINGERS UNDER THE TAIL WILL "ENCOURAGE" HIM TO MOVE OUT WHEN YOU'RE READY!

BOWLINE KNOT

THE RUMP ROPE REALLY IS THE HORSEMAN'S BEST FRIEND! USE A BOWLINE SO THE LOOP WON'T TIGHTEN — THEN WITH GENTLE TUGS ENCOURAGE THE FOAL TO MOVE OUT, GRADUALLY TRANSFER PRESSURE FROM RUMP ROPE TO LEAD ROPE.

AT RIGHT IS AN OLDER COLT BEING GIVEN A LESSON IN LEADING. HE WAS HALTER BROKEN EARLIER BY THE BREAST-HITCH METHOD, AND RESPECTS IT NOW!

months old. By this time the colt should look forward to being handled and will come willingly whenever the trainer appears.

The eventual quiet, well-mannered colt results from slow, unhurried training. When the colt is led for the first time he should be guided along behind his mother. Put the left arm under the neck and the right toward the rump, with two fingers slightly under the tail, using a light pressure to propel the colt forward. Then use the rump rope. Hold the colt by the halter and loop a rope around the rump just above the hocks, holding it together over the back. By grasping the two pieces of rope across the back and pulling slightly on the halter at the same time, the colt will move forward. Sometimes this is all that is needed to teach a colt to lead. If there is difficulty with the rump rope and the colt still does not lead, use a chest rope.

Tie one end of a long rope into a slip knot. At times it may be safer to use a bowline instead of a slip knot, if the animal is excitable. Place the rope over the colt's back and pull the balance of the rope through the slip knot or bowline. Bring this up through the front legs, up through the halter, to make a lead rope. Now, as you pull, the pressure of the chest rope between the colt's front legs will cause him to move forward. Be gentle and give only a slight tug, otherwise the colt will leap forward. For the next few weeks the colt should be led around until there is no necessary pressure on the chest rope or breast hitch. This is also a good time to accustom the colt to being tied. Tie short enough so that the legs will not become entangled in the rope. If the colt should pull back, the pressure of the chest rope on the under arms of the front legs of the colt will cause him to come forward. If you have an old inner tube, tie one end to within a few inches of the colt's halter and the other end a few inches from the tie ring. The colt may pull back, but the elasticity of the tube will give with him and he has less chance of being hurt. The colt will connect the discomfort with pulling back and you will be saved many broken halters. However, the age of the colt is important and also the size animal you are working. Naturally, a large colt will be more difficult to handle than a small one.

Sometimes foals are not handled until weanling time and then you have a hefty colt to handle. The method you use will be determined by the size and gentleness of the foal or weanling you are going to work. If you can get your arms around a foal for the preliminary halter breaking, it will be a simple matter. If the animal is too large for this, then the best method is to adjust the halter and place a chest rope in position. Allow the colt to drag this around for a while and quite a bit of the fight and fear will be gone before the handling. Then you may use a come-along. This is the same as the rump rope but run through the halter, and the trainer stands to the front of the animal. Also, a head come-along can be used. A rope is tied around the neck (bowline knot) and looped over the nose so that the rope comes over the loop. A pull on this rope causes it to tighten, and the colt will discover he is relieved when he steps forward. A heavy cement block in company with an inner tube will take the preliminary starch out of a young animal. The tube gives enough to prevent the animal from injuring itself and yet holds enough for restraint. Every day the colt should be subjected to the method that works best for him.

Each day the colt should be groomed, feet handled and cleaned, led about, and sacked out.

To become a safe animal the colt must learn not to be startled by anything. This is done by sacking out. Hold the lead rope in the right hand and gently slap the colt about the shoulders with a gunny sack. If the animal is uneasy, rub the sack all about his body. When this is tolerated, slap the colt about the legs, then the rump, and, lastly, the head. Proceed with each part of the body only as the colt tolerates the sacking. When at last the colt can be touched anywhere on the body, in any manner, with the sack, he may be considered quite gentle.

Only the lack of maturity prevents the colt from being mounted at six months of age, because a young horse is capable of learning at any age. Discipline is important at any early age, and much can be done by longing. The purpose of longing is to exercise the animal, and is frequently used on mature horses when there is no time for riding. Longing makes the colt flexible and obedient to the voice of the trainer. It teaches him to stop and turn quietly on command. He learns to circle equally well to the right or left on a walk, trot, and slow canter. You will need a long line, leather, canvas, or rope with a snap on one end. The line should be twenty feet long. It can be made or bought, complete with swivel and cavesson. You will also need a driving whip.

Longing is awkward for the beginner and takes much practice. Some animals will work right out, others will have to be worked from a short distance from the halter, gradually letting out the line as the animal understands what is wanted of him. Some animals will work well from one side and have difficulty from the other. This means that the owner must have a mountain of patience. Don't wrap the line around your hand. Let it play out as you need it. The whip is held in the free hand and rotated behind the animal to urge it forward. Place yourself nearer the animal's hip so he will understand he is to go forward. Stop the animal frequently and tell him to come. Start and stop him, using the words "walk" or "trot" as you wish him to change gaits. Most horses learn longing quickly, and the most difficult part is to get the animal to move away from the trainer. Don't allow the animal to play on the longe. If he kicks up his heels, jerk him down sharply to let him know he is working. Sometimes it is wise to longe a horse before climbing on his back. By this time all the play and buck will be out of him and he will be ready to settle down to work.

If the colt is strong enough to begin saddle training as a yearling, the animal will be ready by two years of age for riding at reasonable periods. An animal trained for private use at such a young age will have better legs than the youngster who races on the track as a long two-year-old. Place a small, light saddle on the colt's back and tighten the cinch lightly. The colt should be led around until he becomes accustomed to carrying the saddle on his back. Mounting the colt will depend on his sturdiness and maturity as a yearling. Lean across the colt's back and bounce slightly so the colt will become used to added weight. If the rider does not weigh more than fifty or sixty pounds it will not hurt the legs or the back. It is not the back you must worry about, but the legs. Because of the hard running and the pounding effect on the front legs thoroughbreds raced at two years often break down.

A pleasure horse would not be expected to run in this manner, so that reasonable riding with a little easy cantering would not hurt the young legs. After the experience of the saddle the colt should not object to carrying a child.

When the time is decided upon for riding, no more than ten minutes of riding should be allowed. However, the colt may be ridden three or four times a day for these short periods. After the colt is eighteen months old, twenty minutes is not too long. As the colt becomes accustomed to the weight, then the time limit may gradually be increased. It is better to have two people start the colt under saddle, one in the saddle and one on the ground. The rider should thoroughly understand aids, body cues, and reining. Working together, the person on the ground will pull the colt forward as the rider at the same instant shifts his weight and releases the reins. Every body cue and aid should be exaggerated until the colt learns to move forward.

As the colt becomes accustomed to being ridden the cues will come more naturally and smoothly. Nothing more than starting and stopping should be done the first week of saddle training. Allow the colt to walk about twenty feet, stop, and start again, until the cues are learned. As the colt begins to move on cue, the ground trainer should start to step back, along the lead rope, to give the colt a chance to move by his own volition. When the colt is moving out by cue alone then the second trainer should mount a horse and ride alongside. This will give assurance to the colt and also give him a chance to watch what he must do. Colts also learn by watching other horses. The colt will learn to match his stride with that of the more experienced horse. Then is the time to start neck reining.

Because the colt's mouth is tender, use a hackamore until he is at least three years old. Hold a rein in each hand. In turning to the right, for example, lay the left rein across the neck of the colt and at the same time pull to the right with the other rein. Lean slightly to the right with the body and press with the knee on the right side. You repeat the same, only on the opposite side, for turning left. It takes quite a while for the colt to respond to the reining, so give a lot of time to this part of the training and be patient. Be sure the cuing is right and exaggerated so the colt will "get the feel" of what he is to do. When the colt is walking freely, stopping, and starting, and has a fair rein, then he is ready to trot.

The cue for the trot must be firmer than for the walk. Each gait results from a harder forward motion of the body. By posting the trot, the colt can be taught collection and rhythm. To post correctly, keep time with the front legs. When the right leg lifts, rise in the saddle. When the left leg lifts, sit down. When the post is done correctly, the rider will feel the rhythmic moving of the horse's front legs. Posting is only correct in English riding but it is an excellent way to teach the young horse rhythm in the trot to make it easier to sit the western trot.

By the time the colt is two years old he should be easily managed by an amateur rider providing the rider is instructed to handle the colt the way he has been trained. A rank amateur, pulling and tugging on the reins, can ruin the best-trained colt in a short time.

When the colt is put into the canter, he should lead out

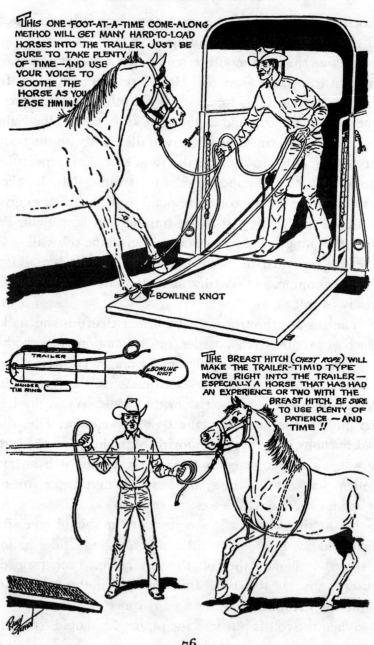

THIS ONE-FOOT-AT-A-TIME COME-ALONG METHOD WILL GET MANY HARD-TO-LOAD HORSES INTO THE TRAILER. JUST BE SURE TO TAKE PLENTY OF TIME—AND USE YOUR VOICE TO SOOTHE THE HORSE AS YOU EASE HIM IN!

BOWLINE KNOT

TRAILER

HANGER TIE RING

BOWLINE KNOT

THE BREAST HITCH (CHEST ROPE) WILL MAKE THE TRAILER-TIMID TYPE MOVE RIGHT INTO THE TRAILER— ESPECIALLY A HORSE THAT HAS HAD AN EXPERIENCE OR TWO WITH THE BREAST HITCH. BE SURE TO USE PLENTY OF PATIENCE—AND TIME !!

with his inside leg. For example, if the colt is going in a circle to the left, he should lead out with the left front leg. The leads have been explained in a previous chapter. Always keep the colt at an even, easy canter. A colt can be made "speed crazy" if he is run at a dead gallop all the time. Frequently retrain your horse, stopping and starting and reining as you did in the beginning. It acts as a refresher course and keeps the animal alert.

Don't go from the trot into a canter. Bring the colt to a walk and then cue for the canter. If this is not done, the colt will always take a few trotting steps before breaking into the canter. To experienced horsemen it gives the impression that the horse has not been well trained. Should you enter a Western Pleasure class at the horse show, you will be marked down for this. Even though you want your horse just for pleasure, never allow yourself or your animal to become sloppy in riding habits.

There will be times when you want to travel a distance with your horse, either for shows or for trail riding. This means that your animal should be well acquainted with a trailer. It is better to train the foal with the mare. The fact that the mare goes into the trailer readily will cause the foal to accept it. If the foal is used to nibbling or eating in the trailer, there is usually no problem. Don't lead the foal in and then right out. The foal will begin to think this is what is expected and will not stay in long enough to close the ramp. Leave the colt for at least twenty minutes with the ramp closed, then before removing the animal reward him with grain. Take the colt for short rides so he will learn to balance.

Practice stopping and starting, a few sudden stops, as

might occur unexpectedly on the road, so the animal will learn to adjust and accustom himself to different trailering conditions. There are many ways of loading if an animal balks at the prospect. Loading a foal or young colt can be done by two men with locked hands behind the rump. The animal is boosted into the trailer. Here again the chest rope may be used. Sometimes a rump rope, fastened to one side of the trailer and the other end drawn across above the hocks, will gently urge the animal forward. Many times an animal may have to be walked in, a foot at a time. Someone holds the animal by a halter rope and the helper lifts first one foot and then another until the horse walks into the trailer a few inches at a time. Most horses, after overcoming their fear, enjoy riding and will walk right into the trailer by themselves when it is time to go.

Bad Habits

Horses acquire bad habits from mishandling, from boredom, spoiling, and fear. Some of the most common faults are cribbing, kicking, shying, balking, rearing, bolting, crowding, starting forward before the rider is settled in the saddle, and being barn soured.

To find the cure it is wise to try to find the cause. An experienced horseman can usually tell what causes a horse to react as he does. Most horses can be retrained unless the animal has been mistreated cruelly or ridden incorrectly over a long period of time. It is seldom that a really vicious horse can be retrained. He has already been disillusioned, he cannot bring himself to trust a man, and the habit of hate is too well established. The odds of even the expert horseman ever making the animal usable are few.

Let's take the faults in the order mentioned and give their cure. A horse that is cribbing will bite on the manger or door or possibly a post. It is said to be caused by indigestion or by the teeth pressing too closely against one another. However, it is certain that an animal stabled next to a cribber will pick up the habit, and once the habit is well established there is a chance he will never get over it. Whatever the cause, it is a disagreeable habit. Horses seldom crib on anything lower than their knees. Remove the manger and feed from the ground for a time. If the habit is new, this may cure it. A habitual cribber may never be cured. However, a horse that chews on wood is not necessarily a cribber. Horses chew on rails and posts when they have nothing to do. When an animal is confined in too small an area he will chew wood. See that the horse gets plenty of exercise and nail metal nosing on all wood rails and on the corners of the posts.

Horses kick out if they're startled. Habitual kicking can be caused by putting another horse into the next stall— the kicker will lash out while eating. Some horses kick just to hear the clatter of their hoofs and some to feel their strength. A spoiled horse will kick whenever he is interrupted. A bully will kick other horses to assert himself. Kicking is a dangerous habit, and should be stopped as soon as noticed. If the animal kicks when you approach, then he should be punished with a sharp cut of the whip administered every time he tries to kick and at the precise moment he is in the act.

If this is not effective, then a foot length of heavy chain attached to a collar and placed just above the hock of the kicking leg will stop this habit in a few days. Horses kick right- or left-handed, so be sure you have the leg the animal habitually kicks with. In this manner he will punish himself and will eventually be afraid to kick, remembering the pain of the chain. After the chain treatment the habit rarely occurs again, but if it does, replace the chain for another treatment. Striking goes in line with kicking. It first starts

as a playful gesture in a colt and then graduates to an expression of anger. A sound whipping across the front legs
is necessary. Don't put it off, as it will get worse.

Most horses, being farsighted and not able to focus on
close objects, will shy at some movement they cannot understand. When a horse shies at something, bring him to it
and let him smell and examine it with his muzzle. Talk to
him in a soothing voice. Learn to recognize the things that
frighten your horse and be prepared to guide him gently
by them. Always be ready for a sudden jump. Very young
or highly strung animals must be watched for shying.
Gentleness must always be used. If possible, when riding,
turn their heads away from the object that frightens them.
If riding with a companion, allow him to go ahead; your
horse will probably follow without fear. A horse that has
confidence in his rider can be quieted by a reassuring word.
Because shying is caused by fear, we should mention
frightened horses.

A frightened horse is an uncontrolled animal. He is like
anything else beset by fear. There is no reasoning power,
nothing but sheer panic. The rider is faced with a quick
decision—whether it is safer on the animal's back or whether
to leave the saddle. If it is open country, possibly the sooner
you can leave the saddle the better. However, if in tight
quarters it is difficult to say. There is danger of being
trampled, kicked, or struck. A horse blinded by fear may
run into a wall, a tree, or rear up and over backward. In a
case of this kind there is little advice to give.

Balking is an aggravating and frustrating habit to come
up against, and the beginning rider is at a great loss to know
what to do. It is sometimes caused by starting the animal

too quickly and then pulling back violently, whipping the horse until he is so confused and excited that the habit of balking is begun. It is also a result of bad schooling. There is a cure, however. Turn the horse in a short circle, about five turns. The animal will be so concerned with dizziness he will forget what it was that made him balk.

Rearing is sometimes a form of balking. It is a result of poor training, hard hands, or poor bitting. It can also be caused by fear. The animal who rears because he doesn't want to leave the stable is bluffing. He rarely rises more than a foot or so off the ground. When a horse rears, prick him good with a pair of spurs. This will usually bring him down. Try this on yourself. Raise your arms above your head and then have someone poke you in the ribs. Rearing can also be stopped by circling, holding the turning rein under the right boot, as this pulls the head downward. Above all, don't pull on the reins or you will pull your horse off balance and over backward. Sometimes a rolled newspaper is effective if used to strike the horse between the ears. Or a plastic bag of water has been suggested, used with the theory that the animal will think it is his own blood trickling down his face. It is certainly most humane, but may have no effect. However, a horse rarely rears when you expect him to, and you might carry a bag of water for a long time before being able to use it. Also, if the rider will throw his weight forward and keep it there, an animal must come to his feet. Sometimes a tie down will prevent the animal from rearing, or at least any great height. A more severe method is tripping. This, however, should not be attempted except by an expert horseman. If you have bought a rearing animal and minor treatment is not effective, take him to a good trainer.

Bolting is a frightening experience even for the expert rider. A horse bolts for many reasons. If may be from fear, or he may have excess energy and wants to go home. First of all, try not to allow the animal to get out of hand. When you put the horse into a canter, see that he maintains the speed you want. If you feel him wanting to run, then try turning him in a circle. Make the circle smaller and smaller until he can be controlled. You may also try bringing the left rein over the neck just in front of the withers. At the same time place the right hand as low down on the off side of the neck as possible and hold him hard in this position. Also, if you are near a hill, try to turn him up the grade. This will usually slow him down. If you are riding with companions, never pursue a runaway horse. If you hear the animal coming up behind you, block the road. However, be careful doing this if the animal should be running blindly. You can usually tell by the animal's eyes whether he is running from fear or orneriness.

If the rider is thrown, turn your own horse back a few steps. Many times a loose animal will turn and follow another horse. If two horses get away from their riders, there is not much to do but walk home. The horse that runs back to the barn is considered barn sour. It is also almost impossible to get him away from the barn. The animal may rear at the time or just refuse to budge. The rider must be ever alert. The animal will seldom try this with an experienced rider. However, circle him until he is dizzy and then head him in the direction in which you wish to go. A nick with the spurs will also convince him to change his mind.

Don't allow the horse to win this fight or you will never leave the barn. Out on the trail a horse does not like to leave a group. It is a good idea to make your horse do everything you wish of him when in a group so he will become accustomed to minding.

It is a common fault for a horse to start away before you're able to swing into the saddle. It is because of poor training but it is easy to cure. Put a few pieces of carrot in your pocket. Hold the reins firmly until you are in the saddle and then reward him with a carrot. Sometimes if you give him a piece before mounting he will wait until you are settled, hoping for more. In this case don't disappoint him. Hobbles placed above the pastern will make moving uncomfortable enough to force the horse to stand. Mount and dismount many times until the animal begins to stand. A few treatments before starting out on a ride will fix the habit. Once a horse is trained to stand for mounting, don't jump into the saddle and jab him with spurs to make him run.

Biting should be taken care of when the horse is a foal. If an animal is teased, he may resort to biting. Slap the muzzle sharply or pinch the lip every time he bites. A young boy bit his pony on the muzzle and the small animal never attempted to bite him again. In wintertime, when the coat is long, a horse will sometimes bite because the hair is pulled by the tightening of the cinch.

A horse that refuses to tie and pulls back on the halter will leave a trail of broken equipment. It is also a sign of poor training. Use the chest rope and leave the animal tied for fifteen minutes at a time. If the animal pulls back, the chest rope will press against the nerves under the front legs, causing such discomfort that the horse will move forward to remove the pressure. A few days of being tied with the chest rope will cure this habit.

Pawing is a noisy habit and will result in holes in the stall and paddock. A horse will paw if confined in a small area when he is hungry or impatient. Treat this habit much as you do kicking. A strap around the leg above the knee with a block of wood fastened on a short rope, hanging about six inches, will hit his shins. Give your horse a large pasture to run in and there will seldom be any pawing.

If a horse is well treated, kept in good health, and has plenty of exercise he will seldom have bad habits. Treat a bad habit as soon as it is noticed or take means to prevent it in the first place. Remove the cause if possible. Keep the animal occupied and satisfied and he will have no time to get into mischief.

Etiquette

Horsemen in general are the most congenial, the most helpful group in the world, but don't like and won't accept phonies. Everyone wants to have the feeling of belonging whenever they join a horse group. A rider may become obnoxious, without meaning to, by the manners he displays and the way he manages his horse around others. To get "off on the right foot" is important. More than likely they have observed the ability of the new horseman and made up their minds as to the type of person he is.

An experienced horseman can tell a true horseman by his actions around a horse, the way he approaches it to mount, the manner in which he picks up the reins. A good horseman proves his ability by action, not by word. An unpardonable sin is to tell anyone what a good horseman you are.

When you first approach a group, introduce yourself, explain where you come from, and that you would like to get acquainted. The conversation will almost immediately lead to your horse. Someone is sure to say, "Pretty nice animal you have there." This is the icebreaker. You can give the group an idea about yourself by explaining the breeding, where you bought him, and what you think he can do, being modest on the latter.

In this first conversation your new acquaintances will know what knowledge of horsemanship you have. "Horse talk" is like any other "trade talk." An engineer can tell another engineer; a plumber, by jargon, knows another plumber, and so on. You can't fool experience. There are definite patterns of behavior you follow with horse people.

You never ask to ride another person's horse, you wait to be invited. It is poor taste ever to ask for anything personal, and a horse is most personal. The fact that an animal can be ruined by poor handling makes an owner cautious about who is allowed astride his horse. If you are in need of an extra horse, rent him from a stable. If you are well known by your crowd, you may be invited to use a friend's horse. But your ability and your respect for the animal will come first. By the same token, don't borrow tack. This includes lead and tie ropes that some owner may have left at the rail while riding. He will expect to find them there when he returns. If you are offered equipment to use, be sure to return it in the good shape in which it was loaned. Defective tack is dangerous, and keeping it in repair is necessary not only for the condition of the equipment but for safety also. Always tie your horse securely when you leave him, and ask permission about where to tie him. If your horse has droppings, when you return you should clean them up. Even if you are astride, perhaps talking to a group, the droppings should be cleaned before you leave. This is a matter of courtesy.

The stable owner has his own work to do, and horsemen,

casually dropping in, can make a lot of work. If you clean up after your horse when visiting, you will always be welcome. Don't be afraid to ask permission about everything you do.

Even on neighborhood trail rides ask permission to accompany a group. Should you have an ill-mannered horse, stay well away from other horses. Don't come to meet new friends "duded up."

For every sport there is proper clothing. You wouldn't think of going swimming in a suit of red-flannel underwear, so don't go riding in a pair of shorts. Western clothing, as other sports clothes, is designed for comfort, for protection, and for style. Don't make remarks about tight-fitting riding pants. Should you ever go on a trail ride with a loose-fitting pair of pants, every wrinkle will form a chafed spot and you will be miserable on the ride and painful for some time afterward. Underwear worn under riding pants should also be form fitting. Jeans, especially because of the roughness of the cloth from which they are made, should fit as tight as comfort will allow. A new pair of jeans will be quite stiff, but a few washings will take the sizing out of the cloth and they will become form fitting and comfortable as they are worn.

Western shirts are designed for rough use and comfort. They fit well about the shoulders and are form fitting about the waist. There is no place for a flapping shirttail when roping calves, bulldogging steers, or even riding a western saddle just for pleasure. A flick of the rope might become entangled with a shirttail and be the cause of an accident. The shirttail could be caught around the horn when dismounting, or be caught up in the reins. The yoke of the shirt gives more freedom to the arms and keeps the shirt from splitting on the sides. The snap buttons are for quick removal of the shirt when necessary. Chaps are not for decoration, either.

Chaps come in many styles, and each has a purpose and use. The primary use for the chap was to protect a good pair of breeches from getting torn by brush, maybe a leg from a bruise or scratch, knees dry and warm in bad weather. Since the introduction of chaps by the Spaniards when they brought their cattle to Mexico they have undergone many changes in style and use. The closed-leg chap, not used much today, was the most practical. It had no superfluous leather, it was light in weight as well as warm, and rainproof. Fur chaps were popular, first, because they shed rain and were windproof, then they became the badge of the rodeo performer. However, they are seldom seen any more. Batwings or flap chaps have been worn since the earliest days and are still preferred by some rodeo performers to enhance their bronco riding. The working cowboy uses them for the added protection when working on the ground. Chinks come just below the knees and are used during hot weather, for light brush, ring showing, and parading. There is the Mexican tight leg or California pants, reinforced with buckskin for a good grip. There are at least thirteen styles of chaps, different belt types, and decorations. As always, styles come and go, and many of the styles are only memories.

Western boots have made almost as many changes. The old western boot had a high heel. This type heel had many uses and was a definite safety feature. It prevented the cowboy from shoving his foot through the stirrup and eliminated being hung up in the saddle if thrown. It was used to "dig in" when holding a calf or a horse. A good pair of western boots will last many years. There is no footwear more comfortable than a well-fitted boot. No matter how long they are worn, nor how frayed the leather becomes, they never appear to stretch out of shape. However, with the popularity of western clothing spreading to non-riders the boot changed to many styles. You may buy a pointed toe, round toe, flat heel, high heel, scallop tops (shallow or deep), stovepipe, and every height from the six-inch to sixteen. Every material from rough out to sealskin, sharkskin, alligator skin, pigskin, kidskin, and horsehide is used. Some boots are even suède Indian type, which can come well up over the knee. Some have zippers. They come in every pattern of stitching and every combination of colors. The flat heel is better for the horseman who must do a lot of walking or working around horses on the ground. Whether the flat heel or riding heel is used is now a matter of personal preference. Every boot is designed for a purpose and should be selected for suitability to this purpose.

Gloves are an important item of western dress. They protect the fingers and palms of the hands from rope burns, blisters, and calluses. Working horses and cattle is hard work, and if the fingers are not protected there is a chance for fractures and sprains. Gloves will give more protection from these than is realized.

The western hat has more uses than just a head covering. Cowboys have used hats for pillows, as well as for watering and feeding their horses. The large brim was intended for protection against wind, rain, and sun. With all these kinds of misuse the hat can be pushed back into shape again. Hats are usually made of a high-quality beaver material and the brims may be from three to five inches, and many heights and styles in the crown. In the earlier days the crowns were built high, thus the ten-gallon hat. Today we have such crown styles as Horseshoe, Cheyenne Roll, Sho-low Special, Stockman, and Laramie Crush. Straw hats have become popular for their coolness and durability. The Oklahoma Bulldogger is rain-resistant, lightweight, and cool, and is an excellent fit. The hats can be of any color. But crowns and colors aside, a good western hat has more importance than just looking stylish. It should fit snugly. Many people laugh when they see a movie cowboy, in a furious fight, never lose his hat. If the hat fits well, a cowboy can ride a fighting bronc, rope a calf, bulldog a steer, and still have his hat when he is finished. A horseman usually wears his hat well down over his forehead.

Even the kerchief is not for decorative purposes. When driving cattle the cowboy uses it to cover his nose and mouth against the dust of the trail. It can be folded into a narrow band and worn around the throat for warmth. It can be used as a dishcloth, a washrag, a towel, coffee strainer, or a tie under the collar for dress.

Spurs are an important item for every horseman. However, one must learn to walk in them and when to use them on the horse. Cowboys wear them for quick action with a horse. A spur-broken horse rarely needs the use of spurs. He hears them, knows they will be used if necessary, and works accordingly. They are used as aids, training and punishing an animal. No one should be allowed to wear them without thorough training in their proper use.

Western clothing is attractive and comfortable. In choosing apparel, fit it to the need. Don't buy extremely fancy clothing unless it is for a specific purpose. Trick riders go in for sequined shirts and riding pants and flashy colors to glamorize their act, but these have no place with the ordinary rider. Somber tones, matched colors, tailored and well-fitted outfits, and last but not least cleanliness in dress, will put you in the right category of the western horseman.

Trail Riding

ONE of the greatest pleasures of owning a horse is riding trails. These may be anything from the bridle path in the park to the winding trails of a mountainside. There are many dos and don'ts to trail riding. Perhaps the most important is that no person who is not a good rider should be allowed on a mountain trail. First, if the person cannot manage his horse he slows down the other riders. Second, the fun of the ride will be spoiled because the inexperienced rider will need constant help. Third, there is danger of accidents because of his inability to handle the horse properly. Trail riding is much different from ring riding, and the animals react differently.

The preparation of the trail ride should start at the stable. There is the matter of distance, time, and the correct equipment. It is presumed that a trail ride will be for one hour or longer. However, it is difficult to take a trail much under two hours at the least. First, the saddle should fit the horse and be well padded with sufficient blankets. The pressure of the saddle on the animal's withers or back will be greater going up or down hills, and extra padding must be placed well under the fork of the saddle to lessen the friction. The girth or cinch should not be too tight. It is better to stop frequently and adjust the cinch than to have it tied too tightly. Rarely does a well-placed saddle slip if there is enough padding. Polyethylene foam-rubber pads are excellent and will almost entirely insure against slipping.

Carry a slicker tied on the back of the saddle for sudden rains. There should always be a tie rope and a lariat in case of trouble. Once on a trail ride the ground, softened by a spring, gave way under a horse's front feet. The rider jumped clear, but the animal went crashing down the slick mountainside, through brush, and finally came to rest, on his back, wedged against a tree. The animal struggled to regain his feet but the ground was too slippery. A few riders climbed down, tied a rope to the almost-hidden pommel of the saddle, and other ropes around the horse to steady him, and pulled him to his feet. He was none the worse for wear and there was only mud on the saddle. If everyone on the ride hadn't carried a rope it would have been extremely difficult to get the animal back on his feet.

One should never go on a trail alone. If there is an accident, as the one mentioned above, there is no help. If it is necessary to dismount, there will be someone to hold the horse. If the horse should get loose, there will be someone to catch the animal. If he should run home, at least you won't have to walk.

The person at the head of the line is ordinarily considered the trail boss, and all others match their animals' stride to his. He will usually set the pace to the slowest animal on the ride. The person bringing up the rear is called the drag. It is his job to call attention to stragglers. It is also the job of the trail boss and the drag to call out if a vehicle wishes to pass. Every rider in the line passes on the word. In riding along a road every rider should stay on the same side. The side will be chosen by the trail boss according to terrain.

Trail manners are important for the safety and pleasure of the others. When passing another rider, don't come up from behind in a fast trot or gallop. Ask permission to pass, and match your gait with his or wait until he pulls over and stops before you go by him. If someone wishes to pass you, pull over and face your horse toward the oncoming rider. Horses will kick in too close quarters. Don't ride too close to the animal in front of you for the same reason. There should be a horse length between each rider. Don't "cluck" to your horse. Your companion's animal may think the cue is for him and react. If you are riding a kicking horse, tie a red ribbon to his tail as a warning.

If it is necessary for any member to dismount, wait until he is mounted again before proceeding. A lone animal is difficult to mount when out of sight of the others. In going through brush or under low-hanging trees don't hold the branch back unless there is some distance between yourself and the following rider. A swinging branch in the face is painful, and if it should strike the horse's face it could cause the animal to bolt.

In passing through a gate, all riders should wait until the entire group has come through before proceeding. Close all gates firmly behind you. Don't trespass on other people's property without permission. Be careful not to cross planted fields. It is usually safe to ride along the fence line or along the edge of a creek. If you find a damaged fence, report it to the owner.

Don't gallop your horse up a hill. If the hill is steep, tack it, going up or down. Make your turns about fifty feet apart or try to follow the contour of the hill and find a natural path if possible. Don't attempt to force your horse to go where footing is unsteady or questionable. Balance on the balls of the feet where the terrain gets rough so the weight will not be directly on the horse's back. Keep the weight well forward so the animal's hindquarters are free to push up or steady the body coming down.

After negotiating a hill the horses should be allowed to rest. Saddles should be checked for loose cinches and blankets should be in place. On a long ride there should be rest periods of five minutes every half-hour regardless of terrain. When stopping for lunch, the horses should be unsaddled, the tack reversed in the sun, and the blankets spread out to dry. The stop should be at least an hour. The horses should be watered after thirty minutes. If a fast canter has finished this stage of the ride, the horse should be checked and, if hot, he should be walked until cool.

Vary the gaits on the trail. Use common sense in cantering on the trail. Don't race around blind curves. Always sit alert in the saddle and be ready if the horse shies. A rabbit dashing across the road, a deer going through the brush, or a snake on the path may frighten some horses. Try to pick a way through heavy brush so as not to scratch your boots and saddle. If the country is extremely rough, chaps should be worn.

The horse should be rope wise. If the trail ride is to include an overnight camp it might be necessary to stake the horse. Hobbles should always be carried. A horse will not usually travel far when hobbled. Hobbles should be placed on the front legs. However, some horses can gallop quite freely with both front legs hobbled, so it may be necessary to hobble a back and a front leg. People talk of ground tying a horse. However, there is a question about the dependability of a ground-tied horse. There is no guarantee that he will not run if frightened or be swayed by an attractive tuft of grass or another horse. In a case of ground tying an animal, the rider should know his horse and use his own judgment as to whether the animal is dependable or not. It might be well to leave ground tying to the movies. However, if you want your horse to ground tie he may be taught by driving a stake into the ground and tying the horse solidly. He must be convinced that when the reins are on the ground he cannot move. The idea also is that if he moves he will step on the reins. This is fine until a smart animal discovers that by turning his head the reins will be out of his way.

Every horse should be trained to carry double, and to allow a bed roll or pack behind the saddle. If it is a hunting trip, then the horse will be required to carry a deer or a mountain lion. The untrained horse will balk at the smell of blood and will refuse to carry the extra weight. Whirling will sometimes make a horse dizzy until he is loaded with a carcass. If you know the horse will be used for hunting, then a course of training should be undergone.

The horse should be subjected to dry hides, dogs, and calves until he does not resist. Use sacks filled with straw, one tied to each side of the saddle. The western trail horse should lead as well behind another horse as when you are leading him on foot. If your animal does not lead well behind another animal, then put on a chest rope and give him a vigorous jerk when you start out. Keep the lead fairly short and don't allow him to wander or crowd the lead horse. He should neck rein well, ground tie, carry double or pack or game. Some old-timers say to rub blood on the horse's nose when packing a deer or other game.

A trail horse should know how to approach a gate to open. And in opening gates he should know the side pass, be able to back straight, guide left or right when backing. The animal side passes when he crowds a gate to close it. He should be hobble or rope wise. He should jump over low objects on cue and walk through water. He should load and trailer well. The western horse is required to know a greater variety of things than any other horse, and to have the intelligence to recognize danger. A good trail horse will not accept questionable footing or a rickety bridge. Many a horseman owes his life and limb to such a horse. And the pleasure of a trail ride will come in the horse's knowledge of these things.

Horse Shows and Gymkhanas

ALMOST everyone who owns a horse will want to show. There are events for all. If you have a finely bred, well-trained horse, you may want to try the Performance and Equitation classes at your local horse shows. Or if you want to have the fun of competing in timed events there are always play days and gymkhanas. A gymkhana is made up of horse games and timed events. Both horse shows and gymkhanas take much practice, but the winning of a trophy or ribbon is compensation for the effort.

Showing your horse requires as much practice as any other sporting event. The competition is great, and you must learn to be a good loser. You can't just be good, you must be better. Showing for performance requires excellent horsemanship and unless the horse is schooled well in these events there is no use in entering. Play days and gymkhanas take good balance and a certain amount of skill and luck. Decide the type of classes that suit the talents of your horse and keep him in that category. An animal that is well collected and well trained should not be used in a race or game that requires the horse to run with abandon. This will cause the horse to be too animated in a Performance Class where collection is essential. By the same token, a fast horse capable of moving around obstacles should not be expected to become thoroughly quiet to show in equitation.

Performance classes consist of Western Pleasure, Trail Class, Stock Horse, and Western Equitation. In these horses are required to walk, trot, and canter on the correct lead, stop abruptly, and work on a reasonably loose rein both ways of the ring. In Western Pleasure, Stock Horse, and Trail Class the horse is judged. In all Equitation classes the rider is judged for hands, seat, perfomance of horse, and suitability of horse for the rider. The stock horse is required to make two rounds in a figure eight to show change of leads, both back and front, three fast sprints, and a collected stop (mouth should be closed), pivots (swinging front legs to left and right, pivoting on back legs), and backing on a loose rein. In a fast stop, if the animal's mouth flies open it means too heavy a hand and the exhibitor will be marked down in points. In the Trail Class the horse goes through certain designated obstacles chosen by the horse show committee. This usually consists of a stock gate, backing through poles laid at an angle, a short hedge for jumping, a water hazard, a bridge, and a trailer. Sometimes a cowhide is added or a burro with rattling pans tied to his back.

At times, in an effort to make the obstacles more difficult, they are changed to unreasonable hazards that no self-respecting animal on a normal trail would accept. It has been said that the average show trail horse is brain-washed when required to follow through these obstacles to the point where he would be dangerous to ride out on a real trail.

For performance classes appointments are important,

even though they count only 25 per cent. The all-over appearance should be neat and attractive. Hat, gloves, kerchief or tie, chaps or chinks, western boots, and spurs are optional. The saddle should be equipped with lariat, hobbles, slicker, and sometimes a sheathed pair of wire cutters. Some of these things may be optional. The saddle and all tack should be in good condition and clean.

Gymkhana events vary greatly with the region. It isn't possible to describe all of them. Some events by the same name are handled differently in widespread areas. For example: Pole Bending on the West Coast would be thus: Six poles, twenty feet apart. The course is one hundred feet long. The rider may pass the first pole on either side and then shall pass successive poles on alternate sides (serpentine), turn the sixth pole, and return in the same manner. A penalty of two seconds is added to the time for each pole knocked down. Touching a pole with the free hand will also impose a two-second penalty. The rider is clocked as he passes the first pole, and the timing shall be done as the horse's nose passes the pole on the return. A good pole-bending horse will change leads around each pole. The time for this event is nine seconds. A variation of Pole Bending, as done in Colorado, is to start at the entry line, run to the sixth pole, then serpentine to the first, back through to the sixth, and then to the finish line.

The Quadrangle Stake Race is around four stakes placed in the form of a twenty-five-yard square. Two stakes in the center form the starting line. A running start is made twenty feet behind the starting line, and the rider is timed as he enters the course between the poles. The first two turns are to the left, then passing down through the center stakes again, and the last two turns are to the right, finishing as the rider passes between the two center poles again. A two-second penalty is invoked for knocking down a stake. Touching a pole with the free hand also invokes a two-second penalty. The time for this event is twenty-two seconds.

For the Boots and Saddle Race someone holds the horse at the opposite side of the arena. The saddle is on the ground beside the horse. At the starting line the contestant stands with boots at his side. At the signal the contestant puts on his boots, races to the horse, saddles the animal, and rides back to the starting line. The saddle must be checked to determine the correct tying of the latigo. The saddle must be placed correctly. If these items are not right the contestant must go back, resaddle the horse, and ride back to the line again. There have been instances when all contestants were sent back to resaddle. This makes the race more exciting.

The Relay Race consists of teams of four riders each. Each contestant has his own horse but one baton per team. The course is to make a run around a designated pole at the far end of the arena, return, and hand the baton to the next teammate. If the baton is dropped, the rider must dismount, retrieve it, and hand it to the next rider. When the fourth rider has returned to the starting line, the scoring is done to see which team has completed the course first.

In the Double Bareback Race your partner waits on the opposite side of the arena. Race, bareback, to this point, dismount, and your partner swings up on the horse and returns to the starting line.

In the Keyhole Race the start is the same as in Pole Bending. A twenty-foot circle is drawn and lime used to make the markings. The keyhole has a four-foot entrance. The starting line is one hundred feet from the entrance. On signal the rider races toward the entrance, enters, turns, and races out again toward the finish line. Stepping on or over lines of the keyhole or circle will disqualify contestant.

Musical Tires requires one less tire than contestants. When the music starts, the riders canter, clockwise, around the ring. When the music stops, the riders dismount and jump into the tires. The riders are required always to go forward so that if one rider is only three feet ahead of a tire when the music stops he must go all around the ring until he comes to the empty tire. When the music begins again, one tire is removed. This continues until all the tires are removed with the exception of one tire and two contestants. Usually the tie is run off by having the riders take their horses to the end of the arena, dismount, and run back, on foot, to the tire. The first contestant to jump inside the tire wins the contest.

Run-Ride-Lead Race. The contestants start from the far end of the field and run to get their horses (held by a helper), ride to the far end of the field, dismount, and lead the horses back to the finish.

Trailer Race. Contestants must have car or pickup with trailer attached and horse inside. Contestants are brought into the ring and lined up evenly. At a signal the driver gets out of the car, removes the horse from the trailer, saddles him, rides to a given point and returns, unsaddles him, and puts the horse in the trailer, gets back into the car, and turns on the lights.

The Egg Race. The contestant races to a pole at the far end of the field, spoon in hand, dismounts and scoops up the egg, mounts, and returns to the starting line. If the egg is dropped, it must be retrieved. Sometimes ping-pong balls are substituted.

Barrel Race. Place as many barrels as there are contestants at the far end of the field. Contestants start mounted, race to their assigned barrel, dismount, "ground tie" (toss the reins to the ground; the horse should remain standing), crawl through the barrel, remount, and race to the finish line.

Balloon Race. Each contestant is given a balloon on a string. When the whistle blows, each contestant tries to see how many balloons he can break before his own is punctured. When a contestant's balloon is broken, then he must leave the arena. The contestant with the last remaining whole balloon wins the trophy.

Old-Clothes Race. Place a row of sacks containing castoff clothing, such as foundation garments, Mother Hubbards, slips, etc., in a line at the far end of the field. The contestants ride to the assigned sack, dismount, dress in the contents of the sack, mount, and return to the finish line.

Water Race. Each contestant is given a bucket and a helper. At the end of the arena is a tub for each team. One contestant fills the bucket and hands it to the rider. The teammate rides with the bucket and empties the contents into the tub. When time is called, the team having the most water in the tub wins the race.

Potato Race. Fill a box with potatoes and place at one end of the arena. Each contestant is armed with a sharpened spear. The rider endeavors to spear a potato and ride the length of the field to deposit the potato in his own box.

The contestant collecting the greatest number of potatoes in a given time wins.

Nightgown Race. This is done with a team of four, one horse and one nightgown to each team. One part of the team holds the horse, two dress the fourth who must ride seventy-five feet away, ride around a pole, and back to transfer the gown to the next teammate. The humor of all races is the excited awkwardness of the contestants and the unpredictability of the horse. None of these events are as easy as they appear, and skill and ability are not always promise of a win.

Some of these events, such as Pole Bending and Stake Racing, require the horse to be trained to run the course. Speed and coordination between rider and mount are important. The age of the horse or rider is of no consequence.

Young riders who want to have fun at horse shows enter these events. Fine equipment is not necessary. The events are usually divided into senior and junior classes so each will be competing with the right age group. Good fellowship and sportsmanship are necessary at any show.

Manners for horses are an important part of any gathering. You are responsible for the actions of yourself and your horse. Obey the rules and follow the directions of the ring steward. Don't lose your temper and take it out on the horse if you don't win. Remember, your horse is "on stage" and is just as nervous, among strange animals, as you are. Gymkhanas are fun, and inspiring. Participate for the experience of competition, and if you're good enough you'll win and start filling your shelves with trophies and ribbons.

Glossary of Terms

Every sport has a list of familiar descriptive words and terms. Some are technical and others are used in ordinary conversation but have definite meanings. Everyone who owns a horse should learn the correct word to use, so other horsemen will understand what is being said. There is no place for a "what-you-may-call-it."

AIDS. Cues given by legs, hands, and action of the body that signal the horse to work.

AGED. A horse over eight. In shows over four is aged.

BARN SOUR. A horse who will not leave the barn or a group of horses.

BARS OF THE MOUTH. The lower jawline. Used to indicate the portion of the jaw between the incisor teeth and molars commonly known as the bit hole.

BATON. A whip. Batons come in various lengths for training.

BREAKING A HORSE. The days of bronc busting are over, except in rodeos. A horse is broke to ride, then trained.

CANTER. Gallop. Sometimes called a lope, preferably a slow run.

COLD JAW. A horse who has been misused with a bit and is now hard mouthed so no bit will work.

THE WESTERN HORSE

COLORS IN HORSES. Beginning with the darkest: black, bay, brown with black markings from the knee down, black mane and tail. May be golden, red-brown, or blood bay. Chestnut, sometimes called sorrel. May be golden, red, liver, or dark red, with flaxen or red mane and tail. Gray—all white horses except a few are born black and turn white with age, hence they are properly known as grays. Roan designates a horse of solid color with a mixture of white hairs in his coat, thus blue roan or red roan. Palomino must be two shades lighter or two shades darker than a newly minted penny. Has pure-white mane and tail without the presence of black hairs. Pinto is Mexican, meaning paint, and refers to a spotted horse. Piebald is a black-and-white spotted horse. Pintos are divided into three categories. The Tobiana is large spotted. An Overo is spotted underneath the barrel, maybe white stockings, blaze, and usually a glass eye. A Morocco is marked with small all-over spots. An Appaloosa is a breed of horse but is noted for his unusual markings. These horses may be solid color with a blanket of spots on the rump. The Leopard Appaloosa is white with black or red rather oblong spots all over the body.

COMBINATION. A horse that will both ride and drive.

COVER. This term is used in breeding. The stallion covers the mare.

DUDE. A person who is ignorant of horses but would like to pretend he knows and dresses the part with exaggeration.

DOG (apology to the canine). A horse disgusted with the human element of life who has decided he will live longer if he follows the line of least resistance and walks no matter if his passenger threatens to kick his ribs in. He refuses to be moved by spur or whip. The expression "dogging along" comes from this type.

DRUGSTORE COWBOY. Dresses the part but stays away from a horse.

GREEN HORSE. One that has been started but has had little training.

GUNSEL. Usually a non-horse owner who thinks he knows all

about horses. His idea of riding is to see how fast the animal can go. He brags about riding bucking horses. Actually he knows a horse has a head and tail and that's all he knows.

HALTER SHANK. A rope that is attached to the halter for the purpose of leading or tying the horse. Also called lead rope.

HAND. Measuring a horse from the withers, along in line with the front leg, to the ground, is done by hands. A hand is four inches. An animal is said to be 14 hands or 13-3 hands.

HIGH HORSE. A spirited animal.

HUMPING HIS BACK. A horse raises his back slightly when he is getting ready to buck.

LONGE. A form of exercise for the horse without a saddle. An animal is put on a long line and walks, trots, and canters in a circle while the trainer stands in the center and directs the changes by voice or baton.

LUGGER. This horse refuses to respond to the bit and just keeps going faster and faster once he is put in a canter.

MUSTANG. The Spanish word meaning "wild or strayed," a wild horse.

NEAR SIDE. Left side of horse.

OFF SIDE. Right side of horse.

PASSENGER. A person who rents a horse and climbs on and sits down. If the animal moves, it is through the animal's desire to change position.

PLEASURE HORSE. A gentle-mannered horse who moves forward on cue, who does not shy or rear or buck, is easy gaited, and can be ridden by women and children.

PONY. A small equine under 14 hands.

SACKING. This is done to gentle a horse and to "sell" him on the idea that anything the owner does will not hurt him.

SADDLE SOAP. A preparation for cleaning tack.

SCHOOLING. To teach leads, tricks, jumping, roping, cutting, and all phases of advanced, specialized types of horsemanship.

SEASON. A mare "in season" is ready to be covered by a stallion. Normally, a mare is in season three to five days about every twenty-one days. This can vary, however.

SHOW HORSE. Any breed, usually purebred, who trailers from one show to another and spends his life being groomed, trimmed, and worked for particular classes.

SPOOKY. A horse who shies at everything. He will jump if you even raise your hand. Some horses spook because they enjoy being frightened.

STAR GAZER. A horse who holds his head too high with his nose thrust out.

SURCINGLE. A girth used with a blanket or pad. It can be made in one piece. It is for bareback riding.

SWITCH TAIL. This is not a good trait in a show horse. It is from faulty training. If an animal is forced faster than he can learn, he switches his tail because he is nervous.

TACK ROOM. A room where tack is kept. Saddles, bridles, etc.

TERMS OF SEX. *Horse:* A mature male over 14-2 hands.

> *Mare:* A mature female.
>
> *Gelding:* A male that has been castrated.
>
> *Foal:* Newly born horse.
>
> *Colt:* A male horse under four years.
>
> *Filly:* A female under four years.
>
> *Stallion:* A mature male.

To FAVOR. To limp.

TRAINING A HORSE. To teach a horse to move forward on cue, to turn left and right, and to back and to stop. To perform in an easy and tractable manner. There is a thin line between breaking and training and schooling as one follows another. Today train is used instead of break because the latter smacks of the "busting-bronc days."

TROT. This is a two-beat gait in which the diagonal legs move together.

TYPES OF REGISTERING. *Purebred:* Both parents are pure of one breed.

> *Crossbred:* Both parents are purebred but of different breeds.

GLOSSARY OF TERMS

Half-bred: One parent is grade or unregistered, the other parent is purebred. Most horse registries have applications for crossbred and half-bred.

Color register: For example: Pinto, Palomino, and Appalousa.

Some horses may be double registered for both color and breed.

WALK. A four-beat gait, free moving. A slow walk is a gait with short strides.

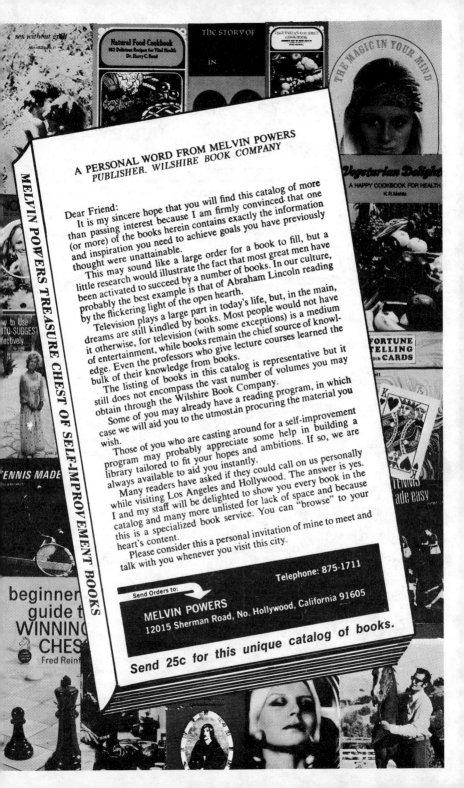

Melvin Powers
SELF-IMPROVEMENT
LIBRARY

ASTROLOGY

——ASTROLOGY: A FASCINATING HISTORY *P. Naylor*	2.00
——ASTROLOGY: HOW TO CHART YOUR HOROSCOPE *Max Heindel*	2.00
——ASTROLOGY: YOUR PERSONAL SUN-SIGN GUIDE *Beatrice Ryder*	3.00
——ASTROLOGY FOR EVERYDAY LIVING *Janet Harris*	2.00
——ASTROLOGY MADE EASY *Astarte*	2.00
——ASTROLOGY MADE PRACTICAL *Alexandra Kayhle*	2.00
——ASTROLOGY, ROMANCE, YOU AND THE STARS *Anthony Norvell*	3.00
——MY WORLD OF ASTROLOGY *Sydney Omarr*	3.00
——THOUGHT DIAL *Sydney Omarr*	2.00
——ZODIAC REVEALED *Rupert Gleadow*	2.00

BRIDGE, POKER & GAMBLING

——ADVANCED POKER STRATEGY & WINNING PLAY *A. D. Livingston*	2.00
——BRIDGE BIDDING MADE EASY *Edwin Kantar*	5.00
——BRIDGE CONVENTIONS *Edwin Kantar*	4.00
——COMPLETE DEFENSIVE BRIDGE PLAY *Edwin B. Kantar*	10.00
——HOW TO IMPROVE YOUR BRIDGE *Alfred Sheinwold*	2.00
——HOW TO WIN AT DICE GAMES *Skip Frey*	2.00
——HOW TO WIN AT POKER *Terence Reese & Anthony T. Watkins*	2.00
——INTRODUCTION TO DEFENDER'S PLAY *Edwin B. Kantar*	3.00
——SECRETS OF WINNING POKER *George S. Coffin*	3.00
——TEST YOUR BRIDGE PLAY *Edwin B. Kantar*	3.00

BUSINESS STUDY & REFERENCE

——CONVERSATION MADE EASY *Elliot Russell*	2.00
——EXAM SECRET *Dennis B. Jackson*	2.00
——FIX-IT BOOK *Arthur Symons*	2.00
——HOW TO DEVELOP A BETTER SPEAKING VOICE *M. Hellier*	2.00
——HOW TO MAKE A FORTUNE IN REAL ESTATE *Albert Winnikoff*	3.00
——HOW TO MAKE MONEY IN REAL ESTATE *Stanley L. McMichael*	2.00
——INCREASE YOUR LEARNING POWER *Geoffrey A. Dudley*	2.00
——MAGIC OF NUMBERS *Robert Tocquet*	2.00
——PRACTICAL GUIDE TO BETTER CONCENTRATION *Melvin Powers*	2.00
——PRACTICAL GUIDE TO PUBLIC SPEAKING *Maurice Forley*	2.00
——7 DAYS TO FASTER READING *William S. Schaill*	2.00
——SONGWRITERS' RHYMING DICTIONARY *Jane Shaw Whitfield*	3.00
——SPELLING MADE EASY *Lester D. Basch & Dr. Milton Finkelstein*	2.00
——STUDENT'S GUIDE TO BETTER GRADES *J. A. Rickard*	2.00
——TEST YOURSELF — Find Your Hidden Talent *Jack Shafer*	2.00
——YOUR WILL & WHAT TO DO ABOUT IT *Attorney Samuel G. Kling*	2.00

CHESS & CHECKERS

——BEGINNER'S GUIDE TO WINNING CHESS *Fred Reinfeld*	2.00
——BETTER CHESS — How to Play *Fred Reinfeld*	2.00
——CHECKERS MADE EASY *Tom Wiswell*	2.00
——CHESS IN TEN EASY LESSONS *Larry Evans*	2.00
——CHESS MADE EASY *Milton L. Hanauer*	2.00
——CHESS MASTERY — A New Approach *Fred Reinfeld*	2.00

_____CHESS PROBLEMS FOR BEGINNERS *edited by Fred Reinfeld*   2.00
_____CHESS SECRETS REVEALED *Fred Reinfeld*   2.00
_____CHESS STRATEGY — An Expert's Guide *Fred Reinfeld*   2.00
_____CHESS TACTICS FOR BEGINNERS *edited by Fred Reinfeld*   2.00
_____CHESS THEORY & PRACTICE *Morry & Mitchell*   2.00
_____HOW TO WIN AT CHECKERS *Fred Reinfeld*   2.00
_____1001 BRILLIANT WAYS TO CHECKMATE *Fred Reinfeld*   3.00
_____1001 WINNING CHESS SACRIFICES & COMBINATIONS *Fred Reinfeld*   3.00
_____SOVIET CHESS *Edited by R. G. Wade*   3.00

COOKERY & HERBS

_____CULPEPER'S HERBAL REMEDIES *Dr. Nicholas Culpeper*   2.00
_____FAST GOURMET COOKBOOK *Poppy Cannon*   2.50
_____HEALING POWER OF HERBS *May Bethel*   2.00
_____HERB HANDBOOK *Dawn MacLeod*   2.00
_____HERBS FOR COOKING AND HEALING *Dr. Donald Law*   2.00
_____HERBS FOR HEALTH How to Grow & Use Them *Louise Evans Doole*   2.00
_____HOME GARDEN COOKBOOK Delicious Natural Food Recipes *Ken Kraft*   3.00
_____MEDICAL HERBALIST *edited by Dr. J. R. Yemm*   3.00
_____NATURAL FOOD COOKBOOK *Dr. Harry C. Bond*   3.00
_____NATURE'S MEDICINES *Richard Lucas*   2.00
_____VEGETABLE GARDENING FOR BEGINNERS *Hugh Wiberg*   2.00
_____VEGETABLES FOR TODAY'S GARDENS *R. Milton Carleton*   2.00
_____VEGETARIAN COOKERY *Janet Walker*   3.00
_____VEGETARIAN COOKING MADE EASY & DELECTABLE *Veronica Vezza*   2.00
_____VEGETARIAN DELIGHTS — A Happy Cookbook for Health *K. R. Mehta*   2.00
_____VEGETARIAN GOURMET COOKBOOK *Joyce McKinnel*   2.00

HEALTH

_____DR. LINDNER'S SPECIAL WEIGHT CONTROL METHOD   1.00
_____HELP YOURSELF TO BETTER SIGHT *Margaret Darst Corbett*   3.00
_____HOW TO IMPROVE YOUR VISION *Dr. Robert A. Kraskin*   2.00
_____HOW YOU CAN STOP SMOKING PERMANENTLY *Ernest Caldwell*   2.00
_____LSD — THE AGE OF MIND *Bernard Roseman*   2.00
_____MIND OVER PLATTER *Peter G. Lindner, M.D.*   2.00
_____NEW CARBOHYDRATE DIET COUNTER *Patti Lopez-Pereira*   1.00
_____PSYCHEDELIC ECSTASY *William Marshall & Gilbert W. Taylor*   2.00
_____YOU CAN LEARN TO RELAX *Dr. Samuel Gutwirth*   2.00
_____YOUR ALLERGY—What To Do About It *Allan Knight, M.D.*   2.00

HOBBIES

_____BATON TWIRLING — A Complete Illustrated Guide *Doris Wheelus*   4.00
_____BEACHCOMBING FOR BEGINNERS *Norman Hickin*   2.00
_____BLACKSTONE'S MODERN CARD TRICKS *Harry Blackstone*   2.00
_____BLACKSTONE'S SECRETS OF MAGIC *Harry Blackstone*   2.00
_____COIN COLLECTING FOR BEGINNERS *Burton Hobson & Fred Reinfeld*   2.00
_____ENTERTAINING WITH ESP *Tony 'Doc' Shiels*   2.00
_____400 FASCINATING MAGIC TRICKS YOU CAN DO *Howard Thurston*   3.00
_____GOULD'S GOLD & SILVER GUIDE TO COINS *Maurice Gould*   2.00
_____HOW I TURN JUNK INTO FUN AND PROFIT *Sari*   3.00
_____HOW TO WRITE A HIT SONG & SELL IT *Tommy Boyce*   7.00
_____JUGGLING MADE EASY *Rudolf Dittrich*   2.00
_____MAGIC MADE EASY *Byron Wels*   2.00
_____SEW SIMPLY, SEW RIGHT *Mini Rhea & F. Leighton*   2.00
_____STAMP COLLECTING FOR BEGINNERS *Burton Hobson*   2.00
_____STAMP COLLECTING FOR FUN & PROFIT *Frank Cetin*   2.00

HORSE PLAYERS' WINNING GUIDES

_____BETTING HORSES TO WIN *Les Conklin*   2.00
_____ELIMINATE THE LOSERS *Bob McKnight*   2.00
_____HOW TO PICK WINNING HORSES *Bob McKnight*   2.00
_____HOW TO WIN AT THE RACES *Sam (The Genius) Lewin*   2.00
_____HOW YOU CAN BEAT THE RACES *Jack Kavanagh*   2.00

_____MAKING MONEY AT THE RACES *David Barr*	2.00
_____PAYDAY AT THE RACES *Les Conklin*	2.00
_____SMART HANDICAPPING MADE EASY *William Bauman*	2.00
_____SUCCESS AT THE HARNESS RACES *Barry Meadow*	2.50

HUMOR

_____BILL BALLANCE HANDBOOK OF NIFTY MOVES *Bill Ballance*	3.00
_____HOW TO BE A COMEDIAN FOR FUN & PROFIT *King & Laufer*	2.00
_____JOKE TELLER'S HANDBOOK *Bob Orben*	2.00

HYPNOTISM

_____ADVANCED TECHNIQUES OF HYPNOSIS *Melvin Powers*	2.00
_____CHILDBIRTH WITH HYPNOSIS *William S. Kroger, M.D.*	2.00
_____HOW TO SOLVE YOUR SEX PROBLEMS WITH SELF-HYPNOSIS *Frank S. Caprio, M.D.*	2.00
_____HOW TO STOP SMOKING THRU SELF-HYPNOSIS *Leslie M. LeCron*	2.00
_____HOW TO USE AUTO-SUGGESTION EFFECTIVELY *John Duckworth*	2.00
_____HOW YOU CAN BOWL BETTER USING SELF-HYPNOSIS *Jack Heise*	2.00
_____HOW YOU CAN PLAY BETTER GOLF USING SELF-HYPNOSIS *Heise*	2.00
_____HYPNOSIS AND SELF-HYPNOSIS *Bernard Hollander, M.D.*	2.00
_____HYPNOTISM *(Originally published in 1893) Carl Sextus*	3.00
_____HYPNOTISM & PSYCHIC PHENOMENA *Simeon Edwards*	3.00
_____HYPNOTISM MADE EASY *Dr. Ralph Winn*	2.00
_____HYPNOTISM MADE PRACTICAL *Louis Orton*	2.00
_____HYPNOTISM REVEALED *Melvin Powers*	1.00
_____HYPNOTISM TODAY *Leslie LeCron & Jean Bordeaux, Ph.D.*	2.00
_____MODERN HYPNOSIS *Lesley Kuhn & Salvatore Russo, Ph.D.*	3.00
_____NEW CONCEPTS OF HYPNOSIS *Bernard C. Gindes, M.D.*	3.00
_____POST-HYPNOTIC INSTRUCTIONS *Arnold Furst*	3.00
How to give post-hypnotic suggestions for therapeutic purposes.	
_____PRACTICAL GUIDE TO SELF-HYPNOSIS *Melvin Powers*	2.00
_____PRACTICAL HYPNOTISM *Philip Magonet, M.D.*	2.00
_____SECRETS OF HYPNOTISM *S. J. Van Pelt, M.D.*	3.00
_____SELF-HYPNOSIS *Paul Adams*	3.00
_____SELF-HYPNOSIS Its Theory, Technique & Application *Melvin Powers*	2.00
_____SELF-HYPNOSIS A Conditioned-Response Technique *Laurance Sparks*	3.00
_____THERAPY THROUGH HYPNOSIS *edited by Raphael H. Rhodes*	3.00

JUDAICA

_____HOW TO LIVE A RICHER & FULLER LIFE *Rabbi Edgar F. Magnin*	2.00
_____MODERN ISRAEL *Lily Edelman*	2.00
_____OUR JEWISH HERITAGE *Rabbi Alfred Wolf & Joseph Gaer*	2.00
_____ROMANCE OF HASSIDISM *Jacob S. Minkin*	2.50
_____SERVICE OF THE HEART *Evelyn Garfield, Ph.D.*	3.00
_____STORY OF ISRAEL IN COINS *Jean & Maurice Gould*	2.00
_____STORY OF ISRAEL IN STAMPS *Maxim & Gabriel Shamir*	1.00
_____TONGUE OF THE PROPHETS *Robert St. John*	3.00
_____TREASURY OF COMFORT *edited by Rabbi Sidney Greenberg*	3.00

MARRIAGE, SEX & PARENTHOOD

_____ABILITY TO LOVE *Dr. Allan Fromme*	3.00
_____ENCYCLOPEDIA OF MODERN SEX & LOVE TECHNIQUES *Macandrew*	3.00
_____GUIDE TO SUCCESSFUL MARRIAGE *Drs. Albert Ellis & Robert Harper*	3.00
_____HOW TO RAISE AN EMOTIONALLY HEALTHY, HAPPY CHILD, *A. Ellis*	2.00
_____IMPOTENCE & FRIGIDITY *Edwin W. Hirsch, M.D.*	3.00
_____JUST FOR WOMEN — A Guide to the Female Body *Richard E. Sand, M.D.*	3.00
_____NEW APPROACHES TO SEX IN MARRIAGE *John E. Eichenlaub, M.D.*	3.00
_____SEX WITHOUT GUILT *Albert Ellis, Ph.D.*	2.00
_____SEXUALLY ADEQUATE FEMALE *Frank S. Caprio, M.D.*	2.00
_____SEXUALLY ADEQUATE MALE *Frank S. Caprio, M.D.*	2.00
_____YOUR FIRST YEAR OF MARRIAGE *Dr. Tom McGinnis*	2.00

METAPHYSICS & OCCULT

_____ BOOK OF TALISMANS, AMULETS & ZODIACAL GEMS *William Pavitt* 3.00
_____ CONCENTRATION—A Guide to Mental Mastery *Mouni Sadhu* 3.00
_____ DREAMS & OMENS REVEALED *Fred Gettings* 2.00
_____ EXTRASENSORY PERCEPTION *Simeon Edmunds* 2.00
_____ FORTUNE TELLING WITH CARDS *P. Foli* 2.00
_____ HANDWRITING ANALYSIS MADE EASY *John Marley* 2.00
_____ HANDWRITING TELLS *Nadya Olyanova* 3.00
_____ HOW TO UNDERSTAND YOUR DREAMS *Geoffrey A. Dudley* 2.00
_____ ILLUSTRATED YOGA *William Zorn* 2.00
_____ IN DAYS OF GREAT PEACE *Mouni Sadhu* 3.00
_____ KING SOLOMON'S TEMPLE IN THE MASONIC TRADITION *Alex Horne* 5.00
_____ MAGICIAN — His training and work *W. E. Butler* 2.00
_____ MEDITATION *Mouni Sadhu* 3.00
_____ MODERN NUMEROLOGY *Morris C. Goodman* 2.00
_____ NUMEROLOGY—ITS FACTS AND SECRETS *Ariel Yvon Taylor* 2.00
_____ PALMISTRY MADE EASY *Fred Gettings* 2.00
_____ PALMISTRY MADE PRACTICAL *Elizabeth Daniels Squire* 3.00
_____ PALMISTRY SECRETS REVEALED *Henry Frith* 2.00
_____ PRACTICAL YOGA *Ernest Wood* 3.00
_____ PROPHECY IN OUR TIME *Martin Ebon* 2.50
_____ PSYCHOLOGY OF HANDWRITING *Nadya Olyanova* **3.00**
_____ SEEING INTO THE FUTURE *Harvey Day* 2.00
_____ SUPERSTITION — Are you superstitious? *Eric Maple* 2.00
_____ TAROT *Mouni Sadhu* 4.00
_____ TAROT OF THE BOHEMIANS *Papus* 3.00
_____ TEST YOUR ESP *Martin Ebon* 2.00
_____ WAYS TO SELF-REALIZATION *Mouni Sadhu* 2.00
_____ WITCHCRAFT, MAGIC & OCCULTISM—A Fascinating History *W. B. Crow* 3.00
_____ WITCHCRAFT — THE SIXTH SENSE *Justine Glass* 2.00
_____ WORLD OF PSYCHIC RESEARCH *Hereward Carrington* 2.00
_____ YOU CAN ANALYZE HANDWRITING *Robert Holder* 2.00

SELF-HELP & INSPIRATIONAL

_____ CYBERNETICS WITHIN US *Y. Saparina* 3.00
_____ DAILY POWER FOR JOYFUL LIVING *Dr. Donald Curtis* 2.00
_____ DOCTOR PSYCHO-CYBERNETICS *Maxwell Maltz, M.D.* 3.00
_____ DYNAMIC THINKING *Melvin Powers* 1.00
_____ GREATEST POWER IN THE UNIVERSE *U. S. Andersen* 4.00
_____ GROW RICH WHILE YOU SLEEP *Ben Sweetland* 2.00
_____ GROWTH THROUGH REASON *Albert Ellis, Ph.D.* 3.00
_____ GUIDE TO DEVELOPING YOUR POTENTIAL *Herbert A. Otto, Ph.D.* 3.00
_____ GUIDE TO LIVING IN BALANCE *Frank S. Caprio, M.D.* 2.00
_____ HELPING YOURSELF WITH APPLIED PSYCHOLOGY *R. Henderson* 2.00
_____ HELPING YOURSELF WITH PSYCHIATRY *Frank S. Caprio, M.D.* 2.00
_____ HOW TO ATTRACT GOOD LUCK *A. H. Z. Carr* 2.00
_____ HOW TO CONTROL YOUR DESTINY *Norvell* 2.00
_____ HOW TO DEVELOP A WINNING PERSONALITY *Martin Panzer* 3.00
_____ HOW TO DEVELOP AN EXCEPTIONAL MEMORY *Young & Gibson* 3.00
_____ HOW TO OVERCOME YOUR FEARS *M. P. Leahy, M.D.* 2.00
_____ HOW YOU CAN HAVE CONFIDENCE AND POWER *Les Giblin* 2.00
_____ HUMAN PROBLEMS & HOW TO SOLVE THEM *Dr. Donald Curtis* 2.00
_____ I CAN *Ben Sweetland* 3.00
_____ I WILL *Ben Sweetland* 2.00
_____ LEFT-HANDED PEOPLE *Michael Barsley* 3.00
_____ MAGIC IN YOUR MIND *U. S. Andersen* 3.00
_____ MAGIC OF THINKING BIG *Dr. David J. Schwartz* 2.00
_____ MAGIC POWER OF YOUR MIND *Walter M. Germain* 3.00
_____ MENTAL POWER THRU SLEEP SUGGESTION *Melvin Powers* 1.00
_____ NEW GUIDE TO RATIONAL LIVING *Albert Ellis, Ph.D. - R. Harper, Ph.D.* 3.00
_____ ORIENTAL SECRETS OF GRACEFUL LIVING *Boye De Mente* 1.00

_____ OUR TROUBLED SELVES *Dr. Allan Fromme*   3.00
_____ PRACTICAL GUIDE TO SUCCESS & POPULARITY *C. W. Bailey*   2.00
_____ PSYCHO-CYBERNETICS *Maxwell Maltz, M.D.*   2.00
_____ SCIENCE OF MIND IN DAILY LIVING *Dr. Donald Curtis*   2.00
_____ SECRET OF SECRETS *U. S. Andersen*   3.00
_____ STUTTERING AND WHAT YOU CAN DO ABOUT IT *W. Johnson, Ph.D.*   2.00
_____ SUCCESS-CYBERNETICS *U. S. Andersen*   3.00
_____ 10 DAYS TO A GREAT NEW LIFE *William E. Edwards*   2.00
_____ **THINK AND GROW RICH** **Napoleon Hill**   **3.00**
_____ THREE MAGIC WORDS *U. S. Andersen*   3.00
_____ TREASURY OF THE ART OF LIVING *Sidney S. Greenberg*   3.00
_____ YOU ARE NOT THE TARGET *Laura Huxley*   3.00
_____ YOUR SUBCONSCIOUS POWER *Charles M. Simmons*   3.00
_____ YOUR THOUGHTS CAN CHANGE YOUR LIFE *Dr. Donald Curtis*   2.00

SPORTS

_____ ARCHERY — An Expert's Guide *Don Stamp*   2.00
_____ BICYCLING FOR FUN AND GOOD HEALTH *Kenneth E. Luther*   2.00
_____ BILLIARDS—Pocket • Carom • Three Cushion *Clive Cottingham, Jr.*   2.00
_____ CAMPING-OUT 101 Ideas & Activities *Bruno Knobel*   2.00
_____ COMPLETE GUIDE TO FISHING *Vlad Evanoff*   2.00
_____ HOW TO WIN AT POCKET BILLIARDS *Edward D. Knuchell*   3.00
_____ MOTORCYCLING FOR BEGINNERS *I. G. Edmonds*   2.00
_____ PRACTICAL BOATING *W. S. Kals*   3.00
_____ SECRET OF BOWLING STRIKES *Dawson Taylor*   2.00
_____ SECRET OF PERFECT PUTTING *Horton Smith & Dawson Taylor*   2.00
_____ SECRET WHY FISH BITE *James Westman*   2.00
_____ SKIER'S POCKET BOOK *Otti Wiedman* (4¼" x 6")   2.50
_____ SOCCER—The game & how to play it *Gary Rosenthal*   2.00
_____ TABLE TENNIS MADE EASY *Johnny Leach*   2.00

TENNIS LOVERS' LIBRARY

_____ BEGINNER'S GUIDE TO WINNING TENNIS *Helen Hull Jacobs*   2.00
_____ HOW TO BEAT BETTER TENNIS PLAYERS *Loring Fiske*   3.00
_____ HOW TO IMPROVE YOUR TENNIS—Style, Strategy & Analysis *C. Wilson*   2.00
_____ PLAY TENNIS WITH ROSEWALL *Ken Rosewall*   2.00
_____ PSYCH YOURSELF TO BETTER TENNIS *Dr. Walter A. Luszki*   2.00
_____ SUCCESSFUL TENNIS *Neale Fraser*   2.00
_____ TENNIS FOR BEGINNERS *Dr. H. A. Murray*   2.00
_____ TENNIS MADE EASY *Joel Brecheen*   2.00
_____ WEEKEND TENNIS—How to have fun & win at the same time *Bill Talbert*   2.00

WILSHIRE MINIATURE LIBRARY (4¼" x 6" in full color)

_____ BUTTERFLIES   2.50
_____ INTRODUCTION TO MINERALS   2.50
_____ LIPIZZANERS & THE SPANISH RIDING SCHOOL   2.50
_____ PRECIOUS STONES AND PEARLS   2.50
_____ SKIER'S POCKET BOOK   2.50

WILSHIRE PET LIBRARY

_____ DOG OBEDIENCE TRAINING *Gust Kessopulos*   2.00
_____ DOG TRAINING MADE EASY & FUN *John W. Kellogg*   2.00
_____ HOW TO BRING UP YOUR PET DOG *Kurt Unkelbach*   2.00
_____ HOW TO RAISE & TRAIN YOUR PUPPY *Jeff Griffen*   2.00
_____ PIGEONS: HOW TO RAISE & TRAIN THEM *William H. Allen, Jr.*   2.00

The books listed above can be obtained from your book dealer or directly from Melvin Powers. When ordering, please remit 25c per book postage & handling. Send 25c for our illustrated catalog of self-improvement books.

Melvin Powers

12015 Sherman Road, No. Hollywood, California 91605

NOTES